A Field Guide to the Information Commons

Edited by
Charles Forrest
Martin Halbert

THE SCARECROW PRESS, INC.
Lanham, Maryland • Toronto • Plymouth, UK
2009

1-9422

SCARECROW PRESS, INC.

Published in the United States of America
by Scarecrow Press, Inc.
A wholly owned subsidary of
The Rowman & Littlefield Publishing Group, Inc.
4501 Forbes Boulevard, Suite 200, Lanham, Maryland 20706
www.scarecrowpress.com

Estover Road
Plymouth PL6 7PY
United Kingdom

British Library Cataloguing in Publication Information Available

Library of Congress Cataloging-in-Publication Data

A field guide to the information commons / edited by Charles Forrest, Martin Halbert.
   p. cm.
  Includes bibliographical references and index.
  ISBN-13: 978-0-8108-6100-8 (pbk. : alk. paper)
  ISBN-10: 0-8108-6100-3 (pbk. : alk. paper)
  ISBN-13: 978-0-8108-6650-8 (ebook)
  ISBN-10: 0-8108-6650-1 (ebook)
  1. Information commons. I. Forrest, Charles, 1953– II. Halbert, Martin.
ZA3270.F54 2009
025.5'23–dc22
                                                    2008039244

∞™ The paper used in this publication meets the minimum requirements of American
National Standard for Information Sciences—Permanence of Paper
for Printed Library Materials, ANSI/NISO Z39.48-1992.
Manufactured in the United States of America.

Contents

Part II: The Field Guide

Information Commons:
A Foreword

Joan Gotwals

The information commons was one of the most significant trends to emerge from developments in the research library community of the late twentieth century. As a conceptual theme that could be adapted to many academic settings, it became a catalytic notion for innovative new library facilities and programs. Librarians, library administrators, academic technologists, and other interested persons will want to understand the range of opportunities presented by the information commons concept. This book, *A Field Guide to the Information Commons*, will provide you with a broad perspective on this trend.

My experience at Emory University illustrates this trend. My first major assignment after arriving on the Emory campus in August 1988 was to chair a committee, appointed by the university president, to determine the central library's future space needs. What new space did the library need to function effectively in the hybrid world of print and electronic information resources and the rapidly changing technology environment? The committee's recommendations called for a new building and upgrading current facilities to serve most effectively the teaching and research needs of faculty and students. It also clearly voiced the desirability of academic computing joining the library in a proposed new building. The report and recommendations were strongly endorsed by the president and provost and this was welcome news to me.

By chance, the newly appointed vice provost for information technology (IT) assumed his new position at the university on the same day that I did. Almost from the beginning, we started exploring ways to work collaboratively in supporting the information needs of the community. After the endorsement of the president for a new building in which academic computing would join the library, the vice provost for IT and I began serious discussions about ways of jointly providing information services and support. Together we began regular meetings with the architects from the firm that was hired by the university. What emerged from these planning sessions was a vision for an integrated service environment, bringing together academic computing, traditional library services, and media support.

In this integrated service environment, students and faculty would have access to information resources of all formats and the members of the community would find a venue there to immerse themselves in a new kind of learning experience. Services and support would come from members of the library's public service units together with those from the academic computing section of the Information Technology Division (ITD), along with those in media production units. We had no desire to merge our two organizations; our aim was to have our organizations work collaboratively in the new building to create "one-stop shopping" for the user. To reflect the expanded role of the library and its partnership with information technology, we called the new building the Center for Library and Information Resources (CLAIR).

While we as leaders of both the library and the Information Technology Division felt strongly about the library and ITD partnership to provide services together, all levels of staff in our two organizations were not always as enthusiastic, especially in the early stages of planning. This was true even though the space in the new building offered academic computing a location at the center of campus for the first time.

The Information Commons was uppermost in our thinking as the key element in the integrated service environment of the new building. We had read about the pioneering efforts at the Leavey Library at the University of Southern California (USC). Since our architects, Shepley Bulfinch Richardson & Abbott (SBRA), were involved in designing the installation there, it frequently came up in our discussions. Library staff visited the USC library and other sites where early versions of the commons concept were in place. We wanted to make sure we learned from those who preceded us in developing an information commons, so we could use their ideas as a foundation on which to build and perhaps add some new features. An issue that was very important in our thoughts and plans was where the Commons was physically located. Our staff members felt that at some sites the Commons was not positioned to be the center of activity, but was off to the side. We wanted the Information Commons to be the central focus, so it would draw patrons to it as they entered the building.

The centerpiece of Emory's new addition, completed and opened in 1998, is clearly the Information Commons. The Commons occupies the central portion of the main level and a large part of the second level of CLAIR. It is a handsome and welcoming gateway into the library and the world of information. The Commons symbolizes the concept of the integrated service environment. The main service point is centered in the midst of clusters of flexible workstations on the main level and is staffed by the library's reference department and support staff from academic computing. Determining staffing for the service desk and ways to manage the Commons, involving the maintenance and replacement of software and hardware, changed over time as we learned from experience and occasional miscalculations. Staff offices for many units of the library, for academic computing, and for media services are located in areas to the rear and side of the Information Commons, so staff members are in relatively close proximity to the Commons.

The term "commons" had great appeal for our staff as we thought of the commons of old and the notion it conveyed of people coming together from all parts of town and sharing ideas and thoughts and perhaps working together on a project. We envisioned a hub of activity, an information hub. We wanted the area to have a sense of energy and excitement about it, with the buzz of an active nerve center, all of which became a reality. As soon as it opened, the workstations in the Commons quickly filled up and the figures for attendance doubled library totals of the past. In fact, according to a survey conducted by a consulting group, the Commons became "the place to be" at Emory. A side effect of its success, however, is a level of noise that sometimes in the evenings becomes cause for concern.

A series of service points makes up one side of the Commons. These service units, consisting of staff from the library, academic computing, or the media production unit, add greatly to the range of information services available. They offer users the opportunity to receive assistance with multimedia resources, to access and manipulate extensive electronic text collections, and to use or create numeric data. The library and technology specialists there assist faculty and students in developing research projects, in creating tools for classroom use, and in working on issues relating to the preservation of digital information, among other topics. Advanced electronic classrooms are available for teaching and may be used to connect to classrooms located around the globe.

We were fortunate in having the right people in the right place at the right time to develop the Information Commons and other new approaches to information support and services. As newcomers to Emory, the vice provost for IT and I both came with fresh ideas about what we needed to do as leaders of the major information providers on campus. We were convinced and determined that only by working jointly in the new electronic environment would we be successful in helping the university achieve its goals for excellence in teaching and research. Our determination to work as a team was demonstrated in many ways. For several years, we even made joint budget presentations and gave joint demonstrations to the university administration to show clearly how technology was changing the ways the library provided services and access to an increasing number of electronic resources. The timing was good in the sense that a major capital campaign was underway at the university, a campaign that focused on the need for new spaces and new approaches for Emory to meet its ambitious goals.

Emory's provost played a key role in keeping library and technology issues highly placed as priorities for the university. Provost Billy E. Frye was a well-known and respected leader in the academic world for his knowledge of research libraries and the impact of technology on academic institutions. He served on various boards at the national level that focused on these matters. His leadership role on the board of the Council on Library and Information Resources, based in Washington, D.C., was especially noteworthy for its strong advocacy for a program to preserve important print collections deteriorating in libraries across the country. For me as a librarian, the prospect of working with him offered a great opportunity.

The Information Commons played a major role in bringing about big changes in the campus community's perceptions of the central library. The library has become "the place to be." It has become a vibrant intellectual center for information gathering and learning, which is all so very different from the situation that I found at Emory when I came in 1988. It is an energized, revitalized central library. Building on long-standing traditions of library service and the more recent partnership with academic computing and media services, the central library has expanded its purview to all forms of information through effective and imaginative use of technology as seen most visibly in the Information Commons. As a result of the electronic environment, with its rich range of services, support, and access in the Commons, plus the strategically developed resources of the Manuscript, Archives, & Rare Book Section, the central library is now able to support the university's goal for excellence in ways that were never possible in depending solely on the print-based collections of the past.

Those who seek to understand how libraries are evolving should read this book carefully to gain insights into academic libraries' embrace of the information commons. The information commons has provided a new programmatic focus for many libraries across the country, and sets the stage for collaborative operations of the future that we have not yet envisioned. I encourage you to delve into this important survey of a significant trend in the history of academic libraries.

Acknowledgments

Charles Forrest and Martin Halbert

A collaborative work like this puts the editors in the debt of many; allow us a moment to single out a few for special mention. We start by thanking our authors, whose contributed essays have so engagingly and effectively described the emergence and evolution of the information commons; we greatly appreciate your effort. Next, our gratitude goes to all those who contributed entries and photos of their information commons; thank you so much.

We would like to acknowledge the efforts of the original information commons implementation team that got the ball rolling for us here at Emory University. Our thanks also go to Joan Gotwals, vice provost and director of the Emory Libraries when Emory's Information Commons was implemented; that your challenge was an inspiration to us is evidenced by the book you (finally!) hold in your hands. Without the unflagging persistence and gentle persuasion of our two graduate student administrative assistants, Carrie Finegan and Robin Conner, this book would never have seen the light of day.

We appreciate the efforts of the team at Scarecrow Press including Blair Andrews, Jayme Bartles, Corinne Burton, and especially Martin Dillon (for becoming a believer).

Finally, we would like to acknowledge the support of our families; you put up with our grumbling longer than you should have, and now you can share in our sense of accomplishment.

Introduction

Charles Forrest and Martin Halbert

"We built some nice new space for computers in the library. Let me show you the lab on the ground floor."

After a short elevator ride with a couple of students, my cheerful and enthusiastic guide and I followed those same students down a short hallway, around a corner, through a door, and into a low-ceilinged space not quite big enough for the rows and rows of computer workstations packed into it.

"We can lock this off from the rest of the library, and operate it on a twenty-four-hour basis," my guide said with a smile. "It's always busy."

"So this is where everybody is," I thought, looking out over the ranks of students, pointing, clicking, and typing away elbow to elbow. "I wonder why they didn't put all these computers upstairs around the Reference Desk, and create an information commons?"

In the past two decades, libraries have responded to rapid changes in their environments by acquiring and making accessible a host of new information resources, developing innovative new services, and building new kinds of spaces to support changing user behaviors and patterns of learning. New forms of technology-enabled information-seeking behavior and scholarship create new possibilities for creating community within higher education, and have drawn a response from libraries that harkens back to the venerable notion of the "commons," a public place that supports conversation and sharing, free to be used by everyone, and which everyone has a right to use, a place that is generally accessible, affable, and familiar.

Without a readily identifiable theoretical wellspring or set of sources, the phenomenon of the "information commons" or "info commons" blossomed in a relatively short amount of time in libraries across North America and around the world, particularly in Europe and the British Commonwealth. The motivation for this book originally came from our own curiosity as we wondered, "What is this phenomenon, and what accounts for its more or less simultaneous widespread appearance?"

A Field Guide to the Information Commons is an attempt to document the emergence of a range of facilities and service programs that call themselves "Information Commons." We here document a snapshot of practice, a range of related new library service models that embody all three of the following spheres of response: new information resources and technologies, collaborative service programs, and redesigned staff and user spaces. While labels have varied widely, the entries of this field guide focus on those institutions that call their integrated service program or facility an "Information Commons," or one of several related terms such as "Technology Commons," "Knowledge Commons," or "Learning Commons." Our aim is not to comprehensively document every occurrence of every form of the commons, but rather, through representative entries, describe how the information commons was actually implemented in libraries across the country and around the world.

The *Field Guide* is structured in two parts. First, a brief series of essays explore the information commons from several perspectives: historical, architectural, and technological, concluding with a case study. The second part is composed of more than two dozen representative entries describing various information commons using a consistent format that provides both perspective on issues and useful details about actual implementations. Later in this introduction, the editors will also provide an overview of our perspective on the conceptual foundations of the information commons as a trend, and our own speculations concerning where this trend in building facilities is going.

The essays provided here bring together a range of perspectives on the emergence of the information commons. Our contributors span many types of professional backgrounds and interests, each offering a different lens on the information commons.

Elizabeth Milewicz examines the "Origin and Development of the information commons in Academic Libraries" in an essay that she developed as part of a larger doctoral research study of library spaces. She contextualizes the information commons movement in a historical perspective of the changing library landscape of the late twentieth century, technological developments in libraries, and what leaders at the time were thinking about the future of library services. Milewicz concludes by capturing the ambivalent reception of the information commons as a central model for future library services, sometimes guarded and sometimes enthusiastic.

Joan Lippincott, in her essay "Information Commons: Surveying the Landscape," gives us the benefit of the many visits she has made over the years to a large number of libraries with information commons programs. She provides a perspective on the variety of interpretations this phrase has taken in different libraries, often meaning significantly different things in different situations.

Carole Wedge and *Janette Blackburn*, architects with Shepley Bulfinch Richardson & Abbott, talk about the need for flexibility in the design of information commons, with an emphasis on designing for new service models and customizing the information commons for increasing breadth and complexity of technologies, services, and resources. They observe that the information commons has expanded far beyond its genesis in library and IT environments, and has come into its own as a distinct type of learning space that accommodates change.

In his contribution, *Richard Bussell* talks about integrating technology into place and purpose and the potential of the commons to connect to print collections and computers, to consolidate online access to information, and to accommodate social learning in an open computing environment. The information commons can support wireless connectivity, provide more advanced technology training, support instruction through faculty production labs, enhance production values in student media productions, encourage experimentation with new instructional technologies, challenge existing uses of technology, and link to campus and global simulation and visualization resources. Bussell asserts that the information commons should provide access to tools and resources that are out of reach of the average student and continually upgrade mainstream technologies, while introducing emerging, potentially disruptive technologies that would otherwise be narrowly defined as specialized research tools.

James Duncan concludes the contributed chapters with a case study of customizing information commons environments in the University of Iowa's Hardin Library for the Health Sciences. He emphasizes the need for a champion for the cause, the ongoing evolution of the commons, the fact that collaboration is core to any commons, and the ongoing requirement to customize physical spaces, create flexibility, and maximize future potential. The information commons can serve as a campus leader, positioning the library as a test bed for teaching and research technologies.

The last word is given to *Crit Stuart*, who encourages us to invite our own students into the process of designing our information commons. If we position our spaces for dwelling, learning, productivity, and socializing, we can revitalize our libraries. Our passion, creativity, hard work, and constant attention to authentic voice and needs of our undergraduates, graduate students, and faculty will inspire us, and enable us to "get it right."

Finally, this essay would not be complete without some commentary by the editors about the remarkable simultaneous emergence of the information commons in so many libraries, and where we see this trend going in the future. First, we believe the confluence of three major contextual factors combined to drive the spontaneous appearance of the information commons over the past two decades in many areas of the country. While each factor may be well known, it was their confluence that led to the discovery of the information commons, accounting for at least some unifying characteristics of this new entity.

Our first broad observation is that user expectations are shaped in the larger social experience outside of libraries. Contemporary culture is highly mobile. Rapid communications and personal mobility ensure that libraries across a broad range of geographical locations will today face a user population with many shared expectations about technology. In addition, user expertise with technology often varies widely. The first factor we would draw attention to is the widespread, rapidly growing, and common experience of new personal computing and networking technologies of most members of society during the past twenty years, but most especially experienced and typically embraced by college-age students. While perhaps obvious and even omnipresent in our attention, this embrace of technology interlinked and interacted with at least two other factors to drive the emergence of the information commons.

Our second observation is that the technological systems commercially available to libraries have been both uniformly available to essentially all libraries, and in fact have *steadily become commodified in price.* When computers became commodified, they went from being unusual purchases by specialized nonlibrary agencies to devices understood as routinely affordable, things that were both capable of being purchased and *expected to be purchased* by libraries, and indeed by most other types of organizations. While libraries have had a particular institutional focus on information, they did not—until recently—have shared expectations of significant or heavy investment in information technology. Libraries now make significant investments in new technologies, perhaps an obvious point by itself, but one which interacted with the other factors to produce an unexpected result.

The final observation that needs to be made is perhaps more subtle, namely that libraries have strong institutional traditions and cultural framing by both librarians and users. Libraries are not culturally empty institutions, but are embedded in a framework of cultural values, assumptions, and judgments. Our claim here is that the core assumptions of value that surround the concept of "library" for both librarians and users have to do with sharing information as a common resource among the members of a community. This is a culturally received concept that is foundational to society's understanding of what constitutes a library. The practical result of this is that *people cannot understand or accept new services as library services if those new services are not conceptually framed by these concepts.*

So in retrospect, it is perhaps not surprising that the phrase "information commons" would seem to capture so perfectly this core cultural framing of libraries, and would be the name of choice independently arrived at by so many libraries as a label for some linked set of new services that deployed information technology in innovative ways. As information technologies and supporting services became increasingly seen and implemented as a normal part of library operations, librarians had to develop a conceptual framework for articulating and presenting such programs to themselves and their clientele. The phrase "information commons" and its variants, such as the "learning commons" or the "technology commons," provide labels to describe a distinctive new program while simultaneously connecting it conceptually to the cultural underpinnings of the library. The variability in the specific programmatic meaning of the phrase "information commons" is neither surprising nor inappropriate. The phrase has a broad and obvious explanatory and evocative sense, while leaving plenty of room for localized and particular interpretations.

This variation in the precise meaning of the term leaves room for relevant interpretation in local settings, while preserving a general sense of the phrase in the larger context. All of the information commons that we have examined have the general attributes of incorporating new technologies and associated services into an existing library setting. Beyond this, we think that it is appropriate that local leaders brainstorm, discuss, and plan what form an information commons should take in their specific settings. Some may focus more on multimedia, others mobile computing; some emphasize facilities, others services.

Local interpretation of the broad information commons concept has not only been the pattern observed to date, but will likely continue as the wholly appropriate way that new high-tech programs are implemented in libraries. When planning a major institutional investment in new services and facilities, careful analysis of local priorities should indeed drive the process, rather than implementation of the specific solutions of other institutions. Having said this, we do think that it is critically important to survey implementations of a range of peer institutions to garner ideas during the initial stages of planning. In fact, it is the general purpose of this book to provide a quick overview of what a range of institutions have done. Combining selective in-person visits to promising locations, with picking and choosing elements that seem to best respond to local needs, will continue to be a most effective way of planning innovative new information commons.

All academic and research libraries face similar challenges and pressures and their responses are conditioned by a shared history and culture. But like politics, all information commons are local. Libraries are usually willing to share and discuss local solutions to common problems, without promoting a single cookie-cutter response. The library is simultaneously a traditional icon for the stability of established knowledge and a leading agent of change for the novel and rapid evolution of today's information landscape. The information commons represents libraries' efforts to bring forward the best elements of both roles in the service of the twenty-first-century user community.

How long will libraries continue to build information commons? While many new facilities continue to be named "Information Commons," the competing term "Learning Commons" has slowly been gaining favor, perhaps indicative of a new emphasis on the expanded role of the library in supporting successful student learning outcomes. But the *common* thread remains the "Commons," emphasizing the role the library has in helping to create and support a viable academic community. We believe that we will continue to see some variant of "Commons" in the names of new endeavors, because there is no other noun that quite captures this idea.

We hope this field guide will suggest some places to look for the information commons, and help you identify the commons when you see it. Whatever similar facilities and programs are called in the future, the information commons has been a rallying point for libraries seeking to reinvent themselves. This trend has had and will continue to have important implications as an evocative new understanding of library services in the future.

I

The Information Commons

1

Origin and Development of the Information Commons in Academic Libraries

Elizabeth J. Milewicz

INTRODUCTION

This chapter highlights twenty years of information commons development in libraries, from its conceptual beginnings in the mid-1980s through the first decade of the twenty-first century. By examining the ideas that led to early innovations in library spaces and contemporary trends, this brief history documents a major shift in the type of space that defines the library and its role in the academic community. This history will consider

- predictions about libraries in the digital age, and how the information commons both challenged and embodied these assumptions;
- technological changes and corresponding pedagogical, professional, and legal trends that contributed to the emergence of the information commons; and
- recent trends that may signal future directions for the nature and role of the information commons in academic libraries.

Though the technology and services in the information commons have expanded over time, its character and emphasis have remained consistent: to provide a collaborative, conversational space that brings together technology, services, tools, and resources to support teaching and learning and encourage innovative ideas. The appellation chosen for these spaces has changed as well, from information commons to learning commons and academic commons, reflecting such shifts in emphasis. In the interest of consistency, this chapter will refer to all such spaces generally as "information commons," with deliberate attention given toward the end to evolutions in these spaces and subsequent changes in name.

THE POWER OF PLACE

In the mid- to late 1980s, just a few years before the first information commons developments, predictions abounded on what libraries of the future would be like. Many librarians and educators agreed that the new libraries would be service-oriented and computer-centered, perhaps merging or collaborating with computer centers.[1] John Budd and David Robinson, attending to predictions of lower college enrollments, proposed that academic libraries could play a more active role in curriculum design and reconfigure traditional patterns of service (including bibliographic instruction) to better accommodate students' needs.[2] In a retrospective article examining the effect of computer technology on library building design, Philip Leighton and David Weber proposed that, as more users accessed resources online, the library space would still retain its value as a learning and work space, offering support services, reference, and other academic assistance, as well as computing space and quiet reading areas for focused study and research.[3]

Others questioned the primacy of the physical building as information became more digital. Professors Lawrence Murr and James Williams asserted that the "'library,' as a place, will give way to 'library' as a transparent knowledge network providing 'intelligent' services to business and education through both specialized librarians and emerging information technologies."[4] Their exposition on the importance of libraries and librarians for managing flows of electronic information emphasized the ethereal library-as-network over the physical library-as-place. Barbara Moran, writing on the fiftieth anniversary of the Association of College and Research Libraries in 1989, predicted that in the near future "users will not have to come to a physical entity, the library, to use its resources."[5]

At the same time, in considering the future of higher education (to which the academic library is obviously and inextricably tied), Moran referenced futurist and philosopher John Naisbitt's observation that the more technology we have, the more we require personal contact with others, and she pondered whether the socializing aspect of these institutions would remain essential.[6] Joan Bechtel's vision of the library as social center struck even closer to the fundamental question of how libraries would meet the demands of a changing information landscape.[7] Calling for a new paradigm of library service, she argued that "libraries, if they are true to their original and intrinsic being, seek primarily to collect people and ideas rather than books and to facilitate conversation among people rather than merely to organize, store, and deliver information."[8]

In many respects, all these predictions were accurate. Throughout much of the 1990s, as the Internet morphed into the World Wide Web, print indexes migrated to CD-ROMs and then online, and OPACs (Online Public Access Catalogs) and databases replaced traditional print resources, libraries witnessed a decline in building usage.[9] Now able to conduct research remotely, many users opted to stay at home or in their offices rather than visit the library. Declines in gate counts, however, plateaued by the end of the century and reversed. Some refer to this as the post-Internet "bounce"—a sign that the initial allure of the Internet had worn off and library users had tempered their irrational exuberance with electronic resources and begun to recognize the enduring value of print.[10] Yet such arguments relegate libraries to a passive role in this process and deeply understate the convenience and appeal of online information. While electronic books have yet to deliver on their promise, faculty and students continue to overwhelmingly select electronic journals and databases over their print counterparts.

What changed was the library itself. The past fifteen years have seen libraries actively reinventing themselves—in the types of resources and services they provide and how they provide them, and in the physical space of the library. In line with many predictions, the new library spaces represent collaboration between librarians and IT personnel and other groups as well. Despite tendencies to downplay the power of place in libraries of the future, some forecasters did predict that libraries would provide an area distinct from typical pedagogical spaces yet offering unique and complementary learning experiences,[11] heralding the information commons spaces that soon materialized.

The information commons visibly and functionally incorporates networked computer resources and collaborative work environments into libraries' mission. It serves as a testing ground for interdepartmental cooperation and shared resources, provides space for different campus populations to meet and collaborate, supports social learning and intellectual play, and reasserts the role of library spaces in fostering and supporting academic work. New pedagogical approaches to knowledge construction in the classroom and a heightened awareness of the role of social spaces in teaching, learning, and scholarship contribute to academics' willingness to experiment in and contribute to these spaces. And some (albeit architects) would argue that the increasing ability to access information electronically, without human intercession, has ironically increased the importance of place as people seek out common spaces for social contact.[12]

WHAT'S IN A NAME?

Understanding what the information commons is and why it emerged is a window into the mind-set of librarians at the fin de siècle, as they faced the future of academic libraries and information access in the digital age and attempted to rearticulate their role in teaching, learning, and scholarship. The phenomenon of the information commons is remarkable not simply for its novelty and its widespread adoption, but also for the cachet of the term itself. The appeal of this label, and the decision by so many institutions to adopt the title for their collaborative work spaces, implies shared beliefs about the role of libraries and informational resources in building knowledge. References to "collaboration" and "community" in library articles in the early 1990s (and that continue to mark discussions in this area) suggest that decisions to renovate and restructure library buildings were predicated in part on egalitarian attitudes toward access to information, ownership of the learning process, and the library's position on campus.

References to "information commons" in legal discussions of access to information, while focused less on physical spaces and more on media ownership, fair use, and other aspects of intellectual property rights, are not unrelated to its use in academic libraries to describe spaces where students, faculty, librarians, IT personnel, and others collaborate and cooperatively construct new knowledge. What began in the mid-twentieth century as a debate about the merits of common ownership of natural resources became by century's end a broader argument about the ownership of information and the importance of information access to democracy.[13] In *The Future of Ideas*, legal scholar Lawrence Lessig draws analogies between the availability and use of electronic information at the turn of the century and the physical commons before industrialization: just as the physical commons provided shared access to resources that people needed to survive and thrive, the information commons or virtual commons provides shared access to the tools, ideas, and instruction needed to perform one's academic work and create new scholarship.[14] While the information commons in libraries represents very literally a physical space, it operates from the same principles as the notion of information commons in legal circles: to encourage the free, collaborative exchange and creation of ideas and information, which in turn benefits and strengthens the community.

Though many institutions chose to call their new collaborative spaces information commons, this history does not exclude from consideration spaces with other names. For instance, the University of Iowa's Information Arcade represents one of the earliest attempts to join new technology and new philosophies of learning within the space of the library. When it was first opened in 1992, the Information Arcade embodied many of the distinctive qualities that have come to be associated with the information commons in libraries:

- embedded and networked computing, information, and multimedia technology that allows users to seamlessly search, access, and apply information in a single location and in a variety of ways;
- flexible or modular architecture that accommodates multiple and divergent activities;
- emphasis on service and instruction through coordinated efforts of a specialized or highly skilled staff; and
- pedagogical philosophies that acknowledge the need for students to take ownership of their learning, rather than receive instruction through traditional means, and to construct knowledge by interacting with others.

The information commons, as both a label and a conceptual ideal, is exemplified by features of the space itself and the philosophy behind its construction more so than by the appellation. Indeed, some "commons" may be so in name only—called information commons or learning commons, and housing computers, yet reflecting little of the larger trend toward collaborative work, community exchange, and technological innovation exhibited in so many of the spaces described later in this guide.[15] For that reason, the information commons may be understood as a type, marked to varying degrees by its conformity to certain principles of social interaction; organizational structure; embedded, ubiquitous, and/or collaborative technology; integration of informational resources and services with processes and tools for teaching and learning; and partnerships between librarians, IT personnel, faculty, and others in creating and supporting these spaces. Though they may differ in the details, information commons typically cohere around the notion that scholarly work is best supported through environments that encourage and are maintained through collaboration, that provide convenient access to the tools, information, and services for accomplishing that work, and that cultivate meaningful interactions among the academic community.

CONTEXTS OF CHANGE

Pedagogical Paradigm Shift

In 1995, Robert Barr, a director of institutional research and planning at Palomar College, and his colleague John Tagg, a professor of English, called attention to a shift that was occurring in higher education—a movement away from the goal of merely providing instruction to a passive, receptive audience to a new focus on fostering learning among active student participants.[16]

> The Learning Paradigm frames learning holistically, recognizing that the chief agent in the process is the learner. Thus, students must be active discoverers and constructors of their own knowledge . . . In the Learning Paradigm, learning environments and activities are learner-centered and learner-controlled. They may even be "teacherless." While teachers will have designed the learning experiences and environments students use—often through teamwork with each other and other staff—they need not be present for or participate in every structured learning activity.[17]

This shift could be seen particularly well in educational literature, where for the past two decades researchers had challenged the traditional structures and processes of pedagogical environments. Referencing the works of such early twentieth-century educational theorists as John Dewey and Lev Vygotsky, these scholars argued that knowledge is not something that passes verbally or visually from teacher to student, but something that must be actively constructed through teacher-student and student-student interactions. They eventually proposed that learning may occur anywhere, at any time, not simply in structured learning environments. For example, Kenneth Bruffee, an English professor at City University of New York's Brooklyn College, emerged as an early proponent of collaborative learning outside the classroom, where students could focus on discussing and solving problems without the pressures of competition, performance, and evaluation.[18]

In essence, this shift in educational theory pushed for new conceptions of the roles and relations of teachers and students and of the where, when, and how of learning. Rather than being relegated to recess, play becomes central to learning: tools critical for conceptual development must be accessible to students outside of structured learning situations and students must be allowed to experiment with them. In addition, students' ability to talk about their ideas with peers emerged as essential for learning. Educators rediscovered Vygotsky's notion of social cognition, which views conceptual development as tightly connected to language.[19] It is not enough for students to be able to repeat a professor's lecture on a topic; they must be able to put these ideas into their own words, to explain them to someone else. In this new paradigm, students take greater responsibility for their learning, the instructor moves from "sage on the stage" to "guide on the side," and the notion of the classroom expands. Further, the emphasis shifts from establishing a heuristic model that all students must fit to creating pedagogical practices that are flexible enough to permit a variety of learning styles and levels.

Previous "instruction paradigm" measures of institutional success, which focused predominantly on the deliverer of the service rather than the receiver, also reflected an understanding of education and educational value as quantifiable.[20] Within libraries this paradigm translated into quality measured by volumes of books, and architectural and organizational planning in turn geared toward the storage of print materials. While the user of the books might be considered in collection decisions and in deciding the number of tables and chairs to provide for reference or reading areas, Vygotskian notions of social learning never entered the equation. For much of the twentieth century, the library building served primarily as a storehouse for books. "People's needs, habits, and learning styles [were] rarely considered in library planning for example, as the ever-growing book stock [was] perceived as the library's contribution to instructional relevancy."[21]

Gradually, this resource-centric approach gave way to a more expansive and inclusive focus. As beliefs shifted about the classroom space and the role of the teacher, so did beliefs about library space and the role of the librarian. Providing computers and other tools and space for academic instruction and student learning became more deeply ingrained in libraries' missions, and new professional organizations emerged to meet this challenge.

Networked Information and Social Learning

The New Learning Communities (NLC) program of the Coalition for Networked Information (CNI) began in the early 1990s as an effort to support student-centered approaches to teaching and learning built upon networked sources of information.[22] Speaking from the perspective of community college libraries, Philip Tompkins, then director of library information services at Estrella Mountain Community College, argued that libraries must find ways to successfully merge print-based and digital cultures and create spaces and services that support interactive learning.[23] Further, libraries must become more integral parts of the teaching-learning experience, integrating instruction and communication into their traditional service of information storage and delivery.[24] Tompkins observed that "an era of reconceptualization and boundary spanning collaboration is occurring":

> This collaboration has implications for telecommunications, microcomputers, the redesign of the classroom and the need for new, sponsored learning environments (spaces) departing radically in design from the theater of the classroom or the traditional library or learning resource center. Above all, a new vision of the role of all campus personnel to accommodate student-centered learning cultures has emerged. It is richly supported by the massing of microcomputer technology and changes in pedagogy. . . . Collaborative and cooperative teaching, and independent, self-paced learning call for new spaces accommodating the massing of newer instructional and information technologies, remote from the theater style classroom. Multimedia ac-

cessibility can usher in changing roles for the instructors who learn to moderate the historic obsession with "telling" to incorporate skillful coaching and facilitating upon call ("from sage on the stage to guide on the side").[25]

Early on, new technologies were linked to new philosophies of teaching and learning, and both would need new spaces to accommodate them. Most librarians saw a shift in the use and structure of library space as an inevitable consequence of new technology; others saw it as an imperative, with the co-location of resources, tools, and services making the library "the public space for scholarship on campus."[26] The ubiquity of personal computers alongside the remote delivery of formerly print-based resources (e.g., library catalogs, indexes, journals, and books) meant that areas once dedicated solely to shelving current periodicals and reference works or housing card catalogs would need to be repurposed or renovated in order to remain viable.

Community colleges, with their instruction-centered and student-focused missions, were primed to adapt their libraries to this new approach. Writing in 1990, Don Doucette of the League for Innovation in the Community College asserted that community colleges would be "the institutions of higher education in which the widespread integration of computers into instructional practices will first take place."[27] Indeed, they were among the first higher education institutions to develop information commons, with several community colleges adopting the model developed by Philip Tompkins.[28]

Despite predictions that top-tier research libraries would resist this expansion in role from resource center to instruction and service center,[29] many major university libraries led the information commons movement, likely because they possessed the funds necessary to develop and maintain these additional tools and services. Indeed, the costs involved in revamping or overhauling infrastructures in order to create an information commons may explain the seemingly lower frequency of information commons development among associate's or baccalaureate/associate's degree-granting institutions.[30]

Connecting People, Places, and Information

The Maricopa County Community College District of Arizona offers one of the earliest-recorded examples of an information commons, with its opening in 1992 of the Estrella Mountain Community College Center, a combined library and technology center "planned as an environment where instructional and information technologies and efforts were to be integrated."[31] From the planning stages, the project sought to leverage new technology for instructional support.

The University of Southern California's Leavey Library, which opened in 1994 but had been in the planning stages for over a decade, also arose from the belief that the library could serve as a link between instruction and technology,[32] and an answer to the information needs of a digital generation of students.[33] When the new library was opened, the director of the Leavey Library stated that he expected the library to be "far more than just a site for information technology and books, far more than just a comfortable place to study and learn. It will be an intellectual center—a place where students and teachers will come to exchange ideas—and I very much want the Leavey to be a center for campus social life as well."[34]

The same year that the Maricopa County Community College District launched its technology and teaching center, the University of Iowa opened the Information Arcade—"a playground for the mind"—that housed a classroom of twenty-four computers and an open independent work area of fifty computers and a few clusters of multimedia workstations.[35] The space was intended to support a range of uses; the electronic classroom was designed to accommodate smaller work groups as well as whole-class discussions. For their part, the faculty often had to restructure their curriculum and pedagogical approach to match the type of teaching and learning supported by the electronic classroom: "As a political science faculty member commented, teaching in the Arcade 'changes the focus. Instead of learning by listening, students learn by doing. It puts me, the teacher, into the role of helping, giving advice. It's a different sort of learning.'"[36]

Besides the novel approach to learning and the diverse array of technology provided within the learning space, another significant hallmark of the University of Iowa's Information Arcade was the collaborative effort involved in producing and maintaining it.[37] Members of the faculty, the libraries, and the academic computing center worked together at the outset to procure funding for the space, and this collaborative approach has continued throughout the life of the Information Arcade.

Joan Lippincott (this volume) observes varying levels of organizational teamwork involved in creating and supporting information commons, from co-location (simply locating different departmental resources services in close proximity) to co-operation (coordinating efforts to provide resources and services), to rare instances of true collaboration (interacting at a deeper level, resulting in shared governance, strategic planning, and goals).[38] In short, though the depth of the relationships may differ, and though in some cases a single campus entity may lead the development, some degree of departmental interaction must occur in order to produce an information commons.

NEW SPACES

Shifting the Focus from Information to Learning

Recent years have seen another stage in the evolution of information commons spaces with the emergence of the learning commons and its sharper focus on creating learning spaces. Some architects and advocates of information commons have begun shifting emphasis from providing networked information sources and services to creating spaces with an array of tools and services specifically designed to foster learning,[39] with particular attention given to the needs of students who have grown up with the Internet.[40]

Some draw careful distinctions between the information commons and the newer learning commons. Whereas the former may be understood generally to provide fluid information access and service delivery, the latter goes a step further by enabling students' effortless orchestration of their own learning tasks.[41] The difference arises not just in a shift in purpose but also in operation: the shape and use of the learning commons is defined and driven by students' learning needs, rather than by the priorities of librarians or computing personnel. Lippincott observes that "a key purpose of an information commons is to leverage the intersection of content, technology, and services in a physical facility to support student learning," but acknowledges that institutions face real challenges in actually facilitating learning.[42] She suggests that information commons may increase their potential for supporting student learning by providing, for example,

- spaces that encourage social interaction and collaboration;
- diverse information formats;
- multiple technologies for accessing and using information, particularly those that students are not likely to own themselves;
- highly skilled and knowledgeable service personnel who can assist students at point of need.

This last point was echoed in the 2006 Canadian Learning Commons Conference, which defined the learning commons as both supporting "numerous aspects of undergraduate and graduate student learning" and, through campus collaborations, "particularly in academic and student services, as well as computing, [providing] a rich array of learning supports."[43] In his keynote address at this conference, Yale University Librarian Emeritus Scott Bennett likewise underlined the pivotal role of collaboration in creating spaces that attend to diverse learning needs.[44]

Rather than signaling a shift in direction, the recent attention to learning heralds a rededication to the partnerships and philosophies on which the information commons was founded. When Donald Beagle summarized the key features of the physical information commons following a decade of development, he pointed to expanded and flexible group and individual study spaces as key to supporting a range of learning styles.[45] Libraries that expand the services and resources provided through the information commons—by adding computer service centers, for example, or writing centers—continue the path set by early information commons developers who sought to support multiple facets of the academic experience, and particularly, to better support teaching and learning.[46]

FROM CULTURAL ICON TO SOCIAL CENTER: CAN A "LIBRARY" BE BOTH?

Likewise, the renewed emphasis on social interaction echoes early hopes that the library would be more than a place to find information and technology by referencing pedagogical beliefs that unstructured, dialogic interactions foster learning. Bennett's call to build spaces that support learning behaviors that are valued by both students and faculty aligns with Lippincott's observation that commons spaces must support social interaction: while the former explicitly orients these spaces toward learning, it also builds on the finding that both faculty and students most value learning behaviors that are built upon conversation.[47] Commenting on trends in library design, university librarian Peter Graham cited the importance of both individual and group study areas at the Syracuse University Libraries: "The library as student center—or, 'coffee shop in the library'—encourages social interaction that tends toward learning."[48] Carole Wedge, an architect involved in the design of numerous information commons spaces, underscores this point, noting that "at Dartmouth, they refer to the library as a 'café with books.' It's the hub of activities after classes, as well as the crossroads of all disciplines."[49] This now widely accepted link between informal social interactions and learning bolsters the incorporation of structures and services that diverge greatly from traditional expectations of what libraries should look and sound like.

Wedge and Janette Blackburn (this volume) expand the information commons category further by introducing the academic commons—a space that goes beyond teaching and learning to provide a staging area for social interactions that connect the campus community.[50] Their discussion of the Undergraduate Learning Center at the Georgia Institute of Technology offers a striking example of this new dimension of information commons space: one intended to support a range of scholarly endeavors, from research to performance to play. Despite the decidedly more informal and high-tech aspects of these new spaces (and in some cases the decision to rename these spaces something other than "library"), Wedge and Blackburn also observe a common desire that these spaces be not simply "cool" and "innovative," but also "majestic" and "memorable."[51]

In some ways, the information commons movement has been successful precisely because it created new spaces in libraries that differed distinctly (in sound and appearance as well as in name) from the established institution. In the early 1990s, when the first of these high-tech computing spaces emerged, some academic libraries perceived a benefit (perhaps even a necessity) in distancing themselves from their long tradition as book repositories:

> To some, the word library became almost a term of opprobrium, as voices—not uncommonly from among college and university trustees, state legislators, and other laypersons—were heard inveighing against the construction of any more outmoded "book warehouses." To change the popular image from one of miles upon miles of bookshelves, some institutions began designating newly constructed library buildings as their "centers for information service," "gateways," or other euphemism instead of "libraries," and indeed perhaps the new terms were more appropriate.[52]

As an egalitarian and decidedly less formal space marked by conversation, the information commons often demonstrates a visual and aural break with the past. Though vaunted by Tompkins and others as a way to bridge the digital-print divide,[53] in practice many of these spaces lean further toward the digital end of the spectrum, with numerous high-tech workstations far outnumbering the available print resources. Furniture, lighting, and even color choices can produce an overall effect of entering a coffee shop or lounge, with conversation levels rising to meet this expectation.

And yet, writing on the future of libraries from the perspective of the twenty-first century, University of Southern California librarian Jerry Campbell recognizes that attempts to change something so revered in academic culture as the library building are bound to meet with resistance.[54]

Early in their history, libraries were endowed by colleges and universities with some of the most beautiful, uplifting, and noble spaces on campus. Usually devoted to reading or meeting, such spaces served and still serve symbolically to reinforce the spirit of learning and to imbue the knowledge-interaction experience with a powerful sense of importance. . . .

Consequently, simply asking questions about the future of libraries, let alone working to transform them for the digital age, almost inevitably evokes anguished, poignant, and even hostile responses filled with nostalgia for a near-mythical institution.

As the information commons enters its second decade, new iterations deliberately reference the more traditional sights and sounds of the library. For example, Indiana University–Bloomington's IC2 continues the trend of previous information commons spaces, with a twist: in addition to computer workstations and wireless access, this new space purports to provide a quiet study environment.[55] Rhodes College has attempted to seamlessly integrate technological convenience with elements of the traditional library. An online description of the building carefully notes that although the library is "a technology center with a theater, complete media production facilities and a teaching and learning center that gives our professors the capacity to hold virtual global classes with colleagues around the world . . . we haven't gone technocrazy. The collection includes books and traditional resources as well as databases and online journals."[56] Along with wireless access, a 24/7 cybercafé, and multiple collaborative study areas "where students can work with professors and each other and actually talk out loud," the library also offers a majestic reading and study room.

Returning to the issue of names, it is noteworthy that there is not consensus regarding the nature of the information commons and the nature of libraries. On the one hand, the term "information commons" was born of necessity, to mark spaces that offered a new and digitally centered research experience. As a product, generally, of collaboration among libraries, IT personnel, and others, there was also a need to mark this space as distinct from the library proper. Consequently, as the information commons concept has gained greater currency and popularity, it has not always carried with it an association with libraries. Though it may structurally support and carry forward a traditional role of libraries—to support scholarly endeavors—the space itself often lacks the traditional features associated with the iconic library building. Systems librarian Martin Halbert's comments on users' initial reception of Emory University's Information Commons illustrate the resistance to calling information commons spaces "libraries":

The Nintendo generation adapts to virtually any and all new dazzling technologies without much ado, but more traditionally oriented generations confront gleaming new computerized spaces with dismay. The problematic response of the latter group is exemplified by a local anecdote about the askance confusion of the grizzled faculty member standing in the (still recognizable, surely!) lobby of the new facility, looking out on a sea of computer terminals (the books stacks are still where they have always been though!) and asking over and over, "Can you tell me, where is the library? I'm trying to find the library. It used to be here." Special care must be taken that new Information Commons facilities do not alienate those users looking for a traditional experience of the library, with all of its delightful textures of marble stairs and mahogany bookcases.[57]

Such sentiments resonate in a recent *Chronicle of Higher Education* commentary on library innovations, as a professor lightly reproaches librarians who replace tactile, traditional research experiences with digital surrogates.[58] Hesitation to conflate the high-tech information commons with the bookish library still persists in some circles, along with efforts to reinstate or emphasize the place of the library building in projecting institutional identity, linking with intellectual heritage, and connecting members of the academic community. Storage of books continues, though increasingly often off-site. If mahogany and marble remain, they may be serving as backdrop or framework for computing, study sessions, and guest lectures, not simply for quiet study and book browsing.

For others, however, "a library by any other name is still a library,"[59] and the information commons, however it may look or sound or act, continues the mission of supporting the scholarly work of the academic community. For architects and librarians alike, the next few decades will determine whether new generations of scholars see libraries and information commons as mutually exclusive, or just two names for the same place.

NOTES

1. Patricia Battin, "The Electronic Library—A Vision of the Future," *EDUCOM Bulletin* 19 (Summer 1984): 13; Richard M. Dougherty, "Libraries and Computer Centers: A Blueprint for Collaboration," *College & Research Libraries* 48 (July 1987): 289–96; C. Lee Jones, "Academic Libraries and Computing: A Time of Change," *EDUCOM Bulletin* 20 (Spring 1985): 9–12; David W. Lewis, "Inventing the Electronic University," *College & Research Libraries* 49 (July 1988): 291–304; Pat Molholt, "On Converging Paths: The Computing Center and the Library," *Journal of Academic Librarianship* 11 (November 1985): 284–88; Barbara Moran, "The Unintended Revolution in Academic Libraries: 1939 to 1989 and Beyond," *College & Research Libraries* 50 (January 1989): 25–41; Lawrence E. Murr and James B. Williams, "The Roles of the Future Library," *Library Hi-Tech* 5 (Fall 1987): 7–23; Raymond K. Neff, "Merging Libraries and Computer Centers: Manifest Destiny or Manifestly Deranged?" *EDUCOM Bulletin* 20 (Winter 1985): 8–12, 16; and Richard L. Van Horn, "How Significant Is Computing for Higher Education?" *EDUCOM Bulletin* 20 (Spring 1985): 8.

2. John M. Budd and David G. Robinson, "Enrollment and the Future of Academic Libraries," *Library Journal* 111 (September 15, 1986): 43–46.

3. Philip D. Leighton and David C. Weber, "The Influence of Computer Technology on Academic Library Buildings," in *Academic Librarianship: Past, Present, and Future: A Festschrift in Honor of David Kaser*, ed. John Richardson, Jr. and Jinnie Y. Davis (Englewood, Colo.: Libraries Unlimited, 1989), 13–29.

4. Murr and Williams, "The Roles of the Future Library," 7.

5. Moran, "The Unintended Revolution in Academic Libraries," 39.

6. Moran referred to John Naisbitt's book, *Megatrends: Ten New Directions Transforming Our Lives* (New York: Warner Books, 1982).

7. Joan Bechtel, "Conversation: A New Paradigm for Librarianship?" *College & Research Libraries* 47 (1986): 219–24.

8. Bechtel, "Conversation," 221.

9. Scott Carlson, "The Deserted Library," *Chronicle of Higher Education* 48 (November 16, 2001): A35–38.

10. Andrew Richard Albanese, "Deserted No More," *Library Journal* 128 (April 2003): 34–36; and Frieda Weis, "Being There: The Library as Place," *Journal of the Medical Library Association* 92 (January 2004): 6–12.

11. Murr and Williams, "The Roles of the Future Library," 7–23.

12. Craig Hartman, "The Future of Libraries," *Architecture* 84 (October 1995): 43–47.

13. Nancy Kranich, *The Information Commons: A Public Policy Report* (New York: Brennan Center for Justice at NYU School of Law, 2004). Kranich cites the following articles as examples of environmental discussions of the commons: H. Scott Gordon, "The Economic Theory of a Common-Property Resource: The Fishery," *Journal of Political Economy* 62.2 (April 1954): 124–42; Garrett Hardin, "The Tragedy of the Commons," *Science* 162 (December 1968): 1243–48; and Anthony D. Scott, "The Fishery: The Objectives of Sole Ownership," *Journal of Political Economy* 63.2 (April 1955): 116–24.

14. Lawrence Lessig, *The Future of Ideas: The Fate of the Commons in a Connected World* (New York: Random House, 2001).

15. Because information commons can vary so widely in appearance, there is a tendency to typify them by their *objects* rather than by their *objectives*, and by foreground appearances rather than background organization. As a cursory definition, Andrew Albanese identifies the key elements of an information commons as "lots of computers, collaborative space, comfortable furniture, and usually some kind of café, lounge, or other suitably social area nearby." Later he discusses a more substantive component: organizational realignments that preceded and supported the information commons' development. Albanese, "Deserted No More," 31.

16. Robert B. Barr and John Tagg, "From Teaching to Learning: A New Paradigm for Undergraduate Education," *Change* 27 (November/December 1995): 12–25.

17. Barr and Tagg, "From Teaching to Learning," 21.

18. Bruffee published a number of articles in *College English* throughout the 1970s and 1980s, arguing for a collaborative learning approach to instruction. See "The Way Out: A Critical Survey of Innovations in College Teaching, with Special Reference to the December, 1971, Issue of *College English*," *College English* 33, no. 4 (January 1972): 457–70; "Collaborative Learning: Some Practical Models," *College English* 34, no. 5 (February 1973): 634–43; "Collaborative Learning," *College English* 43, no. 7 (November 1981): 745–47; and "Social Construction, Language, and the Authority of Knowledge: A Bibliographical Essay," *College English* 48, no. 8 (December 1986): 773–90.

19. Lev Vygotsky, *Mind in Society: The Development of Higher Psychological Processes* (Cambridge, Mass.: Harvard University Press, 1978).

20. Barr and Tagg, "From Teaching to Learning," 12–25.

21. Philip Tompkins, "Information Technology Planning and Community Colleges: A Variance in a Transitional Era" (Report prepared for the *HEIRAlliance Executive Strategies Report #1: What Presidents Need to Know about the Integration of Information Technology on Campus*, 1992), www.educause.edu/ir/library/text/HEI1040.TXT (accessed July 16, 2006).

22. Philip Tompkins, Susan Perry, and Joan K. Lippincott, "New Learning Communities: Collaboration, Networking, and Information Literacy," *Information Technology and Libraries* 17 (June 1998): 100–106.

23. Philip Tompkins, "Quality in Community College Libraries," *Library Trends* 44 (Winter 1996): 506–25.

24. Philip Tompkins, "Quality in Community College Libraries," 506–25; and Philip Tompkins, "New Structures for Teaching Libraries," *Library Administration and Management* (Spring 1990): 77–81.

25. Philip Tompkins, "Information Technology Planning and Community Colleges."

26. David W. Lewis, "Inventing the Electronic University," *College & Research Libraries* 49 (July 1988): 291–304. Lewis quotes John Sack, who spoke during a panel discussion at the Seminar on Academic Computing Services held in Snowmass, Colorado, 1986.

27. Don Doucette, "The Community College and the Computer: Behind Widespread Integration into Instruction," *Academic Computing* 4 (February 1990): 12.

28. Tompkins also helped develop the Information Commons that opened with the new Leavey Library at the University of Southern California in 1994.

29. Van Horn, "How Significant Is Computing for Higher Education?" 8.

30. See, for example, Brookdale Community College librarian David Murray's oft-cited directory of information commons sites, listed by Carnegie Classification. Information Commons: A directory of innovative resources and services in academic libraries, "Sites by Carnegie Classification," Brookdale Community College, www.brookdale.cc.nj.us/library/infocommons/icsites/sitestype.htm (accessed December 8, 2006).

31. Philip Tompkins, "Information Technology Planning and Community Colleges."

32. Doris S. Helfer, "The Leavey Library: A Library in Your Future?" *Searcher* 5 (January 1997): 38–40.

33. Karen Commings, "Inside the University of Southern California's 'Cybrary,'" *Computers in Libraries* 14 (November/December 1994): 18–19.

34. Commings, "Inside the University of Southern California's 'Cybrary,'" 19.

35. Sheila D. Creth, "The Information Arcade: Playground for the Mind," *Journal of Academic Librarianship* 20 (March 1994): 22–23.

36. Creth, "The Information Arcade," 23.

37. Creth, "The Information Arcade," 22–23.

38. Joan K. Lippincott's chapter follows after mine in this volume. "Information Commons: Surveying the Landscape," in *A Field Guide to the Information Commons*, ed. Charles Forrest and Martin Halbert (Lanham, Md.: Scarecrow Press, 2009), 18–31.

39. Donald Beagle, "From Information Commons to Learning Commons" (paper provided for Leavey Library 2004 Conference, University of Southern California, Los Angeles, (September 16–17, 2004), www.usc.edu/libraries/locations/leavey/news/conference/presentations/presentations_9–16/Beagle_Information_Commons_to_Learning.pdf (accessed August 1, 2006); and Scott Bennett, "Righting the Balance," in *Library as Place: Rethinking Roles, Rethinking Space* (Washington, D.C.: Council on Library and Information Resources, 2005), 10–24.

40. Malcolm Brown, "Learning Spaces," in *Educating the Net Generation*, ed. Diane G. Oblinger and James L. Oblinger (EDUCAUSE: 2005), www.educause.edu/LearningSpaces/6072 (accessed August 18, 2006); Joan K. Lippincott, "Developing Collaborative Relationships: Librarians, Students, and Faculty Creating Learning Communities," *College and Research Libraries News* 63 (March 2002): 3; Joan K. Lippincott, "New Library Facilities: Opportunities for Collaboration," *Resource Sharing and Information Networks* 17 (2004): 1–2; Joan K. Lippincott, "Net Generation Students and Libraries," in *Educating the Net Generation*, ed. Diane G. Oblinger and James L. Oblinger (EDUCAUSE: 2005), www.educause.edu/NetGenerationStudentsandLibraries/6067 (accessed August 18, 2006); and Joan K. Lippincott and Malcolm Brown, "Learning Spaces: More Than Meets the Eye," *EDUCAUSE Quarterly* 12 (February 2003): 14–16.

41. Scott Bennett, *Libraries Designed for Learning* (Washington, D.C.: Council on Library and Information Resources, 2003).

42. Joan K. Lippincott, "Linking the Information Commons to Learning," in *Learning Spaces*, ed. Diana G. Oblinger (EDUCAUSE: 2006), 7.6, www.educause.edu/ir/library/pdf/PUB7102g.pdf (accessed November 30, 2006).

43. Canadian Learning Commons Conference, "Towards a Learning Ecology: Canadian Learning Commons Conference Proceedings, June 19–20, 2006," University of Guelph, http://conference2006.learningcommons.ca/ (accessed November 30, 2006).

44. Scott Bennett, "Communication Technology Improvements: Designing in Spite of Uncertainties," in "Towards a Learning Ecology: Canadian Learning Commons Conference Proceedings, June 19–20, 2006," University of Guelph, 2, http://conference2006.learning commons.ca/resources/presentations/proceedings.pdf (accessed November 30, 2006).

45. Donald Beagle, "Conceptualizing an Information Commons," *The Journal of Academic Librarianship* 25 (March 1999): 82–89.

46. With the information commons well into its second decade, many are returning to the question of what students and faculty need and asking whether these spaces are meeting these needs or accomplishing their mission. See, for example, Susan Gardner and Susanna Eng's survey of undergraduates who use USC's Leavey Library. Susan Gardner and Susanna Eng, "What Students Want: Generation Y and the Changing Function of the Academic Library," *Portal: Libraries and the Academy* 5 (2005): 405–20.

47. Bennett, "Communication Technology Improvements," 2; and Joan K. Lippincott, "Linking the Information Commons to Learning." In the proceedings for the 2006 Learning Commons Conference, Bennett lists six learning behaviors most valued by both faculty and students: conversations with students with different values, discussions of readings outside of class, conversations with students of different race, discussions of readings with faculty outside of class, culminating senior experiences, and group study.

48. Jeff Morris, "The College Library in the New Age," *University Business* (October 2002): 28.

49. Morris, "The College Library in the New Age," 29.

50. Carole Wedge and Janette Blackburn's chapter follows later in this book. "Breaking down Barriers to Working and Learning: Challenges and Issues in Designing an Information Commons," in *A Field Guide to the Information Commons*, ed. Charles Forrest and Martin Halbert (Lanham, Md.: Scarecrow Press, 2009), 32–40.

51. Wedge and Blackburn, "Breaking down Barriers to Working and Learning, 39.

52. David Kaser, *The Evolution of the American Academic Library Building* (Lanham, Md.: Scarecrow Press, 1997), 163.

53. Tompkins, "Quality in Community College Libraries," 506–25.

54. Jerry D. Campbell, "Changing a Cultural Icon: The Academic Library as a Virtual Destination," *EDUCAUSE Review* 41 (January/February 2006): 16–31, www.educause .edu/apps/er/erm06/erm0610.asp (accessed August 18, 2006).

55. "Indiana U's IC2," *Library Journal* 130 (May 1, 2005): 15.

56. Rhodes College Barret Library, "About Barret: Our Building," Rhodes College, www.rhodes.edu/barret/2660.asp (accessed August 17, 2006).

57. Martin Halbert, "Lessons from the Information Commons Frontier," *The Journal of Academic Librarianship* 25 (March 1999): 90–91. In the same issue of *The Journal of Academic Librarianship*, Philip Tramdack cautioned of potential conflict between the design of the information commons and users' expectations for library spaces: "Traditional library users may be sympathetic in acknowledging a complex function addressed by the idea of the IC. However, when the design is seen as an alternative to the familiar book-centered and print-bound reference center, anxiety may be the result." Philip Tramdack, "Reaction to Beagle," *The Journal of Academic Librarianship* 25 (March 1999): 93.

58. Fred D. White, "Libraries Lost: Storage Bins and Robotic Arms," *Chronicle of Higher Education* 52 (September 30, 2005): B8.

59. Andrew Richard Albanese, "Campus Library 2.0," *Library Journal* 129 (April 2004): 33.

2

Information Commons: Surveying the Landscape

Joan K. Lippincott,
Coalition for Networked Information

Academic institutions are building or renovating many types of learning spaces, including libraries, computer centers, classrooms, centers for teaching and learning, and multimedia production studios, and they are creating new types of social spaces for student interaction. All of these spaces are relevant to the consideration of the development of information commons in libraries, a phenomenon that began more than ten years ago. This chapter describes the characteristics of an information commons, examines the forces that drive the development of new types of learning spaces, provides examples of existing information commons around the United States and outlines their features, reviews the kinds of services offered and the staff needed to support information commons, and presents a number of current challenges for information commons.

CHARACTERISTICS OF INFORMATION COMMONS

The concept of an information commons is slippery—it means different things in different institutions—and there is no commonly accepted definition among those who manage information commons or those who study them. In fact, some libraries that have space and service configurations that are typical of information commons do not use the terminology to identify their space at all. In simple terms, information commons bring together content, technology, and services in a physical space in order to support the educational mission of the institution. They are planned with the goal of offering a more integrated service environment for users than traditional libraries have provided. From the information commons, users have easy access to library-licensed digital resources (such as databases and electronic journals), the library's print and other collections (such as manuscripts, videotapes, and artifacts), and freely available Internet resources, all from one physical location. This aggregation of information enables users to do their academic work in a way that enhances access to information in different formats. For example, students using books from the library's collection can scan images to use in their papers or presentations, while they simultaneously download articles from library-licensed journals and access websites of nonlicensed materials. This emphasis on availability of content in all formats distinguishes information commons from computer labs.

The technology available in the information commons promotes seamless access to information. For example, high-speed network connections permit users to view streaming video, wireless Internet connections encourage students to use their own laptops, and a range of software enables students to write papers, prepare presentations, or create multimedia products, such as short videos. The variety of software installed on workstations in the information commons typically covers more applications than would be available in a traditional library reference area. Rather than focusing on software applications that only facilitate access to information, the software also supports analysis and management of information and the creation of new information products.

In addition, information commons intentionally provide user services for technology support, as well as services related to content. In most library reference areas, students request technology support, but library staff view these requests as peripheral to the library's service mission. In traditional library areas, staff members are not trained to support a wide array of software applications or to diagnose many technical problems. In contrast, at least a portion of information commons staff is recruited because of their technology skills, and they provide technology support as part of their primary service mission.

As physical facilities, information commons generally consolidate a variety of services into one or more service desks on one floor of the library, supply spaces designed for groups to work with good access to technology, provide comfortable lounge seating in some areas, and offer food and beverages in a café. Some libraries have an information commons on one floor, others have expanded the concept to an additional floor of the library, and others consider the entire library as the information commons. There are few information commons at present that are located outside of the main library; an exception is the Johnson Center at George Mason University, which includes some library services in a student union building, and doubtless there are others, if a broad conceptualization of information commons is used. In addition, there are some information commons in specialized libraries that are housed in classroom buildings that serve specific colleges within a university, such as the University of Iowa Health Sciences Information Commons (see below).

As librarian D. Russell Bailey notes in his survey of the information commons literature, information commons are "library-centric." At their core, they have traditional library content and services, but they also incorporate other elements, such as technology and software, that had formerly been characteristic of computer labs run by campus information technology departments.[1]

The development of information commons was a response to the increased need for the campus community to have access to information technology (networks, hardware, software, and digital content) to accomplish their work. When the first information commons opened in the early 1990s, high-speed Internet access was not generally available campus-wide, fewer students owned their own computers than is the case in the early 2000s, and the amount of scholarly digital content—often licensed by the library and sometimes available only within its walls—was on the rise. Turning some prime library space into an area where students, faculty, and other users could have access to high-speed network connections, large numbers of computers, and digital content seemed to be a winning strategy. Information commons also provided a mechanism for offering library users the kinds of services they increasingly required, such as assistance with computer hardware and software problems.

The information commons movement is also a response to some trends in the higher education environment. As the technology skills of incoming students advanced and their facility with using multiple devices to perform a wide range of activities increased, campuses needed spaces that accommodated the high level of technology use of those students. Providing computer labs was not sufficient for a number of reasons. Students did not necessarily need hardware—they increasingly brought their own laptops to campus—but they needed spaces where they could work and have wireless connections. Students increasingly wanted to work in groups, and the library information commons space was generally reconfigured to offer more group space than had been the case in traditional libraries or computer labs. Students also wanted access to a wider range of software in the library so that they could create their projects as well as access information. As the University of Georgia's Student Learning Center (SLC) states on its website,

> At the SLC, we have a new vision of what a library of the future can be. The SLC is a collaborative learning environment and electronic teaching library. Here, you'll go to class, meet with your friends, work on group projects, study, do research and work on your assignments all in one place! The emphasis is on learning and collaboration and providing you with the tools to make that happen.[2]

Similarly, the mission of the University of Iowa's information commons, called the Information Arcade, is "to facilitate the integration of new technology into teaching, learning, and research, by promoting the discovery of new ways to access, gather, organize, analyze, manage, create, record, and transmit information."[3]

During the late 1990s, many campuses expected a widespread change from traditional teaching methods to technology-enabled methods, but that has generally not happened. Factors such as faculty reluctance to change, small numbers of technology-equipped classrooms, lack of understanding of the relationship of technology to pedagogical goals, and insufficient staff support of faculty, both in preparation of new types of teaching materials and in assistance with equipment and software in the classroom, have slowed this transition from traditional methods. Even though many faculty members do not use technology to a great degree in their classrooms, students use technology in a variety of ways in support of their learning. For example, students use course websites and course management systems, access electronic reserves, search for information via the web or library catalogs and databases, employ software (such as spreadsheet programs or GIS [geographic information systems]) that is relevant to their major disciplines, embed visuals and audio in their papers, and create presentations, websites, and short videos as class projects. Much of student learning occurs outside the classroom, and libraries have traditionally been a venue where students (and faculty) could broaden their learning outside of the classroom's confines. To support today's students' learning styles, libraries can provide technology-rich environments, such as information commons, which offer physical spaces for collaborative work, expert assistance, technology, and content.

EXAMPLES AND FEATURES

With the current wide-ranging discussion of information commons, one would think that they are the prevalent configuration in academic libraries today, but that is not the case. There are a growing number of information commons in American universities and colleges, but more are in the planning stage than have been implemented. For example, in an Association of Research Libraries survey in which seventy-four (60 percent) of their member libraries responded, only twenty-two (30 percent of the respondents) replied that they have an information commons in the library.[4] Many institutions are in the planning phase for developing information commons, generally as part of a library renovation or library renovation/expansion. In some cases, entirely new libraries are being planned that will incorporate an information commons as a key feature.

There are so many variations of information commons that it is difficult to devise distinctive categories that describe identifiable types. However, when examining an information commons, some of the features that may distinguish types include: type of academic institution (or subunit such as an academic department); renovation or new construction; inclusion of services from information technology, writing center, and others; inclusion of multimedia production; and types of group space, including small-group rooms, informal seating, cafés, and classroom space.

This section provides a selective "tour" of information commons, designed to represent those that have received particular attention in the profession and also to represent information commons that have distinctive features or that are in different types of academic institutions. In fact, some of the facilities described here are not even called information commons, but they share many of the features that define the concept of a commons. The "tour" is not intended to be comprehensive, and details provided here will likely change in future years. After all, flexibility and change are essential to the success of any information commons. The examples and features highlighted here help to illustrate the range of institutions creating information commons and differences in these spaces over time and across institutions, components and characteristics frequently identified with information commons, and the wide variation that makes categorizing information commons problematic.

COMPONENTS OF AN INFORMATION COMMONS

- Individual workstations
- Workstations that accommodate small groups
- Group study rooms equipped with computers or space for laptops and projectors
- Practice presentation rooms
- Multimedia production areas
- Rooms equipped with adaptive technology
- Rooms equipped for videoconferencing
- Classrooms for information literacy instruction
- General purpose classrooms for campus use
- Teaching and learning center
- Consultation areas (offering student or faculty consultation with reference librarians, writing tutors, etc.)
- Scanning stations, printer stations, digitization facilities
- Service desk(s) that offer library and information technology assistance or other services, such as laptop or camera loans or computer sales
- Staff offices
- Informal, comfortable seating areas
- Collaboration spaces with specialized software
- Cafés

In the early 1990s, the planners of a new undergraduate library at the University of Southern California realized that they wanted to create a new type of facility that would integrate technology and group learning spaces into the library in innovative ways. The University of Southern California Leavey Library houses what is generally considered one of the first, full-service information commons; it celebrated its tenth anniversary in 2004. It incorporates many features that are now considered standard in information commons in the new millennium. The information commons, originally one floor of an undergraduate library that opened in 1994, includes many more public computer workstations than was common at that time and features a service desk model in which individuals from both library and information technology units are available to provide assistance to users. A number of small-group rooms are available. Today, this information commons continues to thrive. It now includes classroom facilities and offers a practice presentation room, which is equipped with a podium, "audience" chairs, and a computer, projector, and screen setup so that students may practice their class presentations in front of their friends prior to a formal class presentation. A second floor of the Leavey Library has been reconfigured in the information commons style to accommodate more users.

Another early example, called the Information Arcade, opened on the main floor of the library at the University of Iowa in 1992.[5] The Arcade offers workstations, a technology classroom, multimedia production facilities, equipment loans, scanning, and a small-group room. This early inclusion of multimedia production facilities is notable; whether or not to include multimedia production capabilities continues to be one of the key decision points in planning an information commons. Services offered include assistance with library resources and technology. In addition, in-depth consultation is available and extensive support is provided to some faculty or staff projects that focus on using sophisticated or innovative technology in an academic setting.

Some of the large research universities have developed information commons that not only bring together library and computing services, but also incorporate other campus units that serve students. These more collaborative information commons generally involve remodeling one or more floors of the main campus library. The traditional library print collection and other services are typically available on other floors of the facility. Two such projects that have received attention in recent years are the information commons that is part of the Integrated Learning Center at the University of Arizona, and the Information Commons at Indiana University. Both of these projects were planned as joint library/information technology facilities. At the University of Arizona, the information commons has a wide variety of seating arrangements that accommodates both groups and individuals. In addition to various seating configurations in the open areas, including curved counters that offer flexible seating for individuals and small groups and large tables that accommodate multimedia production equipment, there are a number of small-group rooms, information literacy classrooms, and areas where other campus units, such as the writing center, can offer services. Unlike many computer labs built in previous decades or computers in traditional library reference areas, the furniture available in the information commons provides students with room to spread out books, notebooks, and other materials at their computer workstations. The University of Arizona Integrated Learning Center included both renovation of existing space and underground expansion into new space.

At Indiana University, the West Tower of the first floor of the main library was reconfigured into an information commons that offers a large number of workstations—also situated so that individuals and small groups can work comfortably—as well as classrooms, adaptive technologies, a multimedia production area, and a large, central service desk staffed jointly by the library and information technology units. Writing tutorial services are also available. To allow for flexibility in the future, no ceiling-height walls were used in the facility, including around the classroom areas. A second information commons was added on a separate floor, and it is designated as a quiet area.

In a recently opened facility at the University of Massachusetts, Amherst, a number of campus units, such as the career center and the writing center, offer services in the Learning Commons space. There is a central service desk staffed by library and IT staff. A reference desk staffed by reference librarians, with an adjacent office for in-depth, by-appointment consultations, is located nearby.

The Commons at the University of Tennessee, Knoxville library opened in 2005. It includes a practice presentation room with an interactive SMART board like those available in many classrooms around campus. This information commons was developed in existing library space in a very short time frame, as was the information commons in the University of Massachusetts, Amherst library. Like

Arizona, Indiana, and Massachusetts, the Commons at Tennessee was carved out of existing space in the main library.

A different model was developed at the University of Georgia, whose Student Learning Center is one of the few new buildings surveyed that has an information commons as a major component. It is a full-service facility that offers reference service, technology assistance, workshops, tutoring, writing center help, classrooms, group and individual workstations, areas for quiet study, a café, and a project and presentation development room. Library facilities and services are one component of a building that includes many general use classrooms. The main library collection is housed in its traditional home in a separate location.

In recent years, some small colleges have reconsidered their students' technology and learning needs and completely renovated their library spaces or built new buildings. At Middlebury College, a small, liberal arts institution, an entirely new library building opened in 2004. This new building houses the center for teaching, learning, and research, which includes offices for the tutoring program, writing center, first-year program, and others. Its main floor includes reference and help desks, a media lab, and a café. While these are all typical features of an information commons, Middlebury does not use that terminology to describe its facility. The Information Commons at Dickinson College is another small college example. This renovation of library space includes open space computing areas, an area of group workstations that can also be used as a classroom, and an electronic classroom.

A small number of campuses have developed information commons in departmental or program libraries. The University of Iowa Health Sciences Information Commons opened in 1996. James Duncan, former head of the Commons, describes it as "the premier central and delivery venue for health sciences courseware development, innovative classroom instruction, health-related research, and independent learning at the University of Iowa."[6] The facility offers workstations, classrooms, multimedia production facilities, a case-based learning conference room, and production services. Another specialized facility is a small Learning Commons at the Peabody Library at Vanderbilt University, which serves the College of Education and Human Development; it offers public workstations and classroom facilities. These are small-scale models of the information commons found in the main libraries of major research universities.

SERVICES AND STAFF

The core services that libraries provide to information commons users are library information and reference service and technology assistance. Information commons frequently have a service desk that is staffed jointly by individuals from the library and from information technology. The library staff may include librarians, nonlibrarian full-time or part-time staff, and students. Information technology staff may include full-time or part-time staff (who have experience in staffing help desks or similar units), and students. In some cases, libraries retain separate reference desks; in others, all reference work is centralized in the information commons service desk. In some information commons, library and IT staff are cross-trained to answer common questions. In others, library staff address questions related to finding information, locating materials, and library policies, while information technology staff address questions related to the network, hardware, software, or authentication. Workshops on library and technology subjects are sometimes offered as part of the services of the information commons.

In addition to these core services, some information commons rely on individuals skilled in the use of multimedia equipment and specialized software packages to provide support for multimedia production. At the Georgia Institute of Technology's Library West Commons, graduate student assistants receive intensive training from both library and information technology departments, and staff the multimedia production area of the information commons during the busy evening hours. The situation at Georgia Tech exemplifies an ideal asserted by librarian Donald Beagle and realized in only a small number of institutions: "The Information Commons creates a synergy between the user support skills of computer staff, the information skills of reference staff, and production skills of media staff. Physically, it offers the flexible work space all staff need to apply their combined expertise adaptively to the rapidly changing needs of a highly demanding user community."[7]

Other types of services typically offered in information commons include laptop loan, digital and video camera loan, and supply sales (usually through a vending machine). Food and coffee are often sold in a café setting within or near the information commons. The presence of cafés in libraries reinforces the social, community-building nature of the interactions fostered in the commons.

Information commons will continue to evolve as new hardware and software emerge, as patterns of use shift, and as resources are made available. The University of Washington undergraduate library has successfully competed for student technology fee funds to add new services to their information commons, including an audio recording studio and TeamSpot, a large display that allows several users to connect their laptops and collaborate in real time.

Few institutions have developed a coherent set of virtual services that directly support information commons users. For example, many information commons lack specific web pages that describe available services and identify ways to virtually connect to them. While many institutions have instituted chat-based reference services and e-mail services, there is no particular emphasis on using those services from information commons locations. Promotion of virtual services might be helpful, for instance, in busy facilities, where students are often reluctant to leave their workstations to go and ask for help because they may be bumped by other students looking for vacated spots. One issue that is raised in many information commons, even those with several hundred workstations, is how to do a better job of informing students where unoccupied computers are located. At Emory University, an online service alerts information commons users of the availability of workstations on each floor of the library.

Some information commons are planned to co-locate additional campus services into the facility or to provide satellite services in the information commons. Some of these services include the campus writing center, tutoring programs, adaptive technology units, career services offices, academic computing units that focus on research support for faculty, computer sales, and centers for teaching and learning that support faculty efforts to improve their teaching through the use of technology. The University of Massachusetts, Amherst, the University of Arizona, and Indiana University are examples of institutions that have incorporated a number of campus services into their information commons. The overarching concept is to provide users with one-stop, convenient access to services by combining services at a single desk (e.g., library information and computer help), or by bringing additional services into the library building in order to offer them under the same roof but at separate desks or offices (e.g., writing or tutoring programs).

CO-LOCATION, COOPERATION, COLLABORATION

The term collaboration is often used very loosely to describe any type of working together of various parties, but in the management literature, it has a much more precise meaning. Bringing various units that are administratively separate from the library into the physical location of the information commons is frequently referred to as an example of collaboration. However, the presence of these other units may merely be one of convenience or of superficial interaction with the library. If one thinks of a continuum of co-location, cooperation, and collaboration, it may assist planners to think through the type of working relationships and partnerships they might want to establish within an information commons.

In the planning phase, the notion of bringing together a number of campus services is generally one of co-locating services to provide convenience to the user population, especially undergraduate students. Students who need help writing papers or preparing presentations may require assistance from writing center staff who can assist them with the mechanics of writing, from library staff who can aid them in locating information resources, or from information technology staff who can assist them with any hardware or software problems they encounter. Co-location provides convenience to users, but it does not imply the creation of new services that leverage the joint expertise of more than one type of professional group. Co-location of services also provides opportunities for informal staff contact across sectors, especially to encourage easy referral to appropriate service points. When services are co-located, each unit generally has a physically separate service point (a desk or designated area) within the information commons.

In some information commons, the staff of various separate units move beyond co-location to genuinely cooperate in some ways. Cooperative activities can include joint planning for service hours, establishing the scope of each other's work in order to minimize overlap in services, sharing publicity or marketing efforts, and developing centralized workshop schedules. This type of cooperation can lead to increased understanding among units that results in developing an overall plan for services and filling gaps in service offerings. In addition, cooperative efforts can lead to the personnel in the units learning about each other's expertise and being able to make better referrals and plan new types of services.

Few information commons have realized the potential of developing fully collaborative services among unit partners. In collaborative efforts, the units involved would demonstrate that they

- develop *shared* goals;
- engage in joint planning;
- share governance or administration;
- pool expertise to develop new services;
- contribute resources, such as space, staff, or equipment.

For example, if the library had a collaborative relationship with a center for teaching and learning in the information commons, library staff and the center staff would establish goals and create programs to help faculty develop new curricular materials that involve technology and digital content.

Librarians at the University of Tennessee, which has had several successful library/information technology collaborations, suggest that there are readiness criteria by which institutions can judge their capacity to engage in a genuinely collaborative project. These criteria include:

- "culture" (encouraged to innovate);
- history of collaboration;
- executive support;
- willingness to reallocate funds—"bootstrap";
- ability to leverage existing expertise (library and IT).[8]

INFORMATION COMMONS CAMPUS PARTNERS INCLUDE

- library (usually lead partner)
- information technology (usually lead partner)
- faculty academic computing center (research computing)
- center for teaching and learning
- writing center
- career center
- academic advising

CHALLENGES

Some institutions have carefully framed a mission or a set of goals for their information commons, but others have assumed the "if we build it, they will come" philosophy. In fact, students will generally flock to newly remodeled, technology-rich spaces, especially if many of the spaces have been configured for groups. Those institutions that do develop a mission statement generally link the purpose of the information commons to the enrichment of the teaching and learning experience on campus. Developing programming or actively promoting the synergies provided by the physical facility of the information commons, the content available (both traditional and new media), and learning opportunities is the unique value of positioning this facility within the library.[9] It requires careful planning of both the facility and its services to develop direct connections between the information commons and the learning experiences of its users and then to demonstrate the role that the information commons has played in learning. Some library administrators whose institutions have information commons that are packed with students every night are concerned that those spaces have become group study halls with little connection to the content or services of the library.

As part of an assessment process, a group of stakeholders, including librarians, information technologists, instructional technologists, faculty, and students, could discuss and describe some ways that an information commons could enrich the teaching and learning experiences for the institution, and then develop mechanisms for measuring whether or not those expectations were being met. This process could help those responsible for the information commons to carefully think through the services that they offer and the way that they communicate the information commons' unique value to students and other users.

On a broader scale, it is important to develop an assessment program that allows the parties responsible for the information commons to demonstrate the facility's value to library or university administrators or outside funders. Along with documenting use of the facility and services, assessment can demonstrate how that use is linked to desired institutional goals, such as curricular goals (e.g., more integration of technology into curriculum) or social goals (e.g., developing a sense of campus community). Gathering data on what is important to users and what changes they would like to see in the facility and services is another assessment goal.

Many institutions have devoted little attention to promoting and advertising the information commons. Institutional web pages frequently contain little or no information on information commons, and what is available is often difficult to locate. In the libraries themselves, some institutions use large banners to advertise the existence of the commons. While some believe that marketing is unnecessary because so many of these facilities are used at capacity, the purpose of marketing is to promote the kinds of content and services that could enhance the teaching and learning experience of users. For example, default screens of information commons computers could be used to advertise services, mouse pads could include messages that promote digital content at the library, and large screens could display examples of student projects or faculty curricular materials that have been developed as a result of the content and technology available in the information commons. Today's students are especially responsive to visual cues, and information commons staff members should think of creative ways to engage users visually.[10]

Institutions should begin to discuss many of the issues that they will face in operating and maintaining the commons during the planning phase. Many of the individuals and committees involved in planning efforts understandably focus on concrete concerns such as floor plans, furniture, and equipment. Other considerations, such as staffing, staff training, and types of services to be offered, are equally important. Many of these issues can be explored prior to the facility's opening. The overall plan for what services will be offered and by whom is a very important concern. Years or months before the opening of an information commons, libraries can begin to experiment with new service models whereby, for example, users are given support in the production of new media information objects. Libraries can gain a better understanding of what staff are required to support new services and/or what training existing staff may need. If more than one administrative unit—for example, the library and information technology units—will jointly offer services, memos of understanding can be developed to delineate responsibilities and terms.

Information commons are often planned primarily to address students' needs. Faculty needs for support of teaching and learning or research are not as well addressed. Some facilities do incorporate a separate teaching and learning center, which assists faculty with incorporating technology and other pedagogical strategies into their courses. However, these teaching and learning centers often are not well integrated into the services that librarians and information technologists offer in the information commons.

Opening an information commons in a library often requires the library staff to rethink some of their existing policies. Many information commons allow food and drink in their facilities as one means of enhancing the social nature of the space. The ramifications of this policy are the need for increased maintenance and trash pickup, which should be planned in advance of the opening of the facility. At some institutions, the noise level in the information commons disturbs some users. At Indiana University, the staff addressed this issue of students needing advanced technologies in quiet settings by opening a second information commons, designated as quiet space, on a different floor. Other policies that administrators should consider include cell phone usage and restrictions on what equipment can be used for (e.g., computer games or business operations). Involving campus leaders, such as members of student government, in the establishment of policies for information commons is a useful strategy for gaining student input into issues.

Since information commons are, by nature, technology-rich environments, they need regular refreshing. The budget should provide for regular equipment and software upgrades, and staff members must have access to regular training. By design, most information commons accommodate relatively easy reconfiguration of the physical space and service points to allow the library to respond with agility to changing needs.

CONCLUSION

Information commons have been created to support student learning and faculty's capabilities to teach with technology, to provide both individual and group areas for users to access and produce a wide range of information objects, and to offer a broad array of user-centered services. They offer physical spaces, often open for extended hours, in which the institutional community can locate information, access software and high-speed networks, plug-in computers, borrow equipment, and receive assistance from trained staff. They facilitate the type of informal, experiential group learning that appeals to many of today's students.

The information commons phenomenon has existed for a little more than ten years, and it is escalating at a rapid pace. Libraries have the opportunity to create spaces that provide technology-rich environments, encourage the use of scholarly content, and offer knowledgeable staff that can help faculty and students with their academic work. By providing the campus with community-oriented physical space that has academic values at its core, the library can reinforce its valuable role within the institution.

RELEVANT URLS

http://library.gmu.edu/libinfo/jcl.html [Johnson Center at George Mason University]

www.slc.uga.edu/students.html [University of Georgia Student Learning Center]

www.lib.uiowa.edu/arcade/#null [University of Iowa Information Arcade]

www.usc.edu/libraries/locations/leavey/ic/ [University of Southern California Leavey Library]

www.ilc.arizona.edu/features/infocom.htm [Integrated Learning Commons at the University of Arizona]

http://ic.indiana.edu/ [Indiana University Information Commons]

http://commons.utk.edu/ [The Commons at the University of Tennessee, Knoxville]

www.umass.edu/learningcommons/ [University of Massachusetts, Amherst, Learning Commons]

www.middlebury.edu/academics/lis/lib/ [Middlebury College Library]

http://lis.dickinson.edu/Technology/Public%20Labs/Information%20 Commons/index.html [Information Commons at Dickinson College]

www.lib.uiowa.edu/commons [University of Iowa Hardin Health Sciences Information Commons]

www.library.vanderbilt.edu/peabody/commons/ [Peabody Library Learning Commons at Vanderbilt University]

www.lib.washington.edu/ougl/ [University of Washington undergraduate library]

http://infocommons.emory.edu/usage.php [workstation usage alert at Emory Information Commons]

NOTES

1. D. Russell Bailey, "Information Commons Services for Learners and Researchers: Evolution in Patron Needs, Digital Resources and Scholarly Publishing" (paper presented at INFORUM 2005: 11th Conference on Professional Information Resources, Prague, May 24–26, 2005), www.inforum.cz/inforum2005/prispevek.php?prispevek=32.

2. University of Georgia, "Student Learning Center," www.slc.uga.edu/students/library.html.

3. University of Iowa, "Information Arcade: Mission/Overview," www.lib.uiowa.edu/arcade/about/mission.html.

4. Leslie Haas and Jan Robertson, *The Information Commons*, SPEC Kit 281 (Washington, D.C.: Association of Research Libraries, July 2004).

5. Anita K. Lowry, "The Information Arcade at the University of Iowa," *CAUSE/EF-FECT* 17, no. 3 (1994): 38–44.

6. James M. Duncan, "The Information Commons: A Model for (Physical) Digital Resource Centers," *Bulletin of the Medical Library Association* 86, no. 4 (1998): 576.

7. Donald Beagle, "Conceptualizing an Information Commons," *Journal of Academic Librarianship* 25, no. 2 (1999): 88.

8. Barbara Dewey and Brice Bible, "Relationships and Campus Politics in Building the Information Commons" (paper presented at Academic Libraries 2005: The Information Commons. NY3Rs Association and the Academic and Special Libraries Section of NYLA. Saratoga Springs, N.Y., November 11, 2005), www.ny3rs.org/al2005.html.

9. Joan K. Lippincott, "Linking the Information Commons to Learning," in *Learning Spaces*, ed. Diana G. Oblinger (Boulder, Colo.: EDUCAUSE, 2006), www.educause.edu/LearningSpaces.

10. Joan K. Lippincott, "Net Generation Students and Libraries," in *Educating the Net Generation*, ed. Diana G. Oblinger and James L. Oblinger (Boulder, Colo.: EDUCAUSE, 2005), www.educause.edu/educatingthenetgen/.

3

———◆———

Breaking Down Barriers
to Working and Learning:
Challenges and Issues
in Designing an
Information Commons

Carole C. Wedge and Janette S. Blackburn,
Shepley Bulfinch Richardson & Abbott

BREAKING BARRIERS BY DESIGN

As designers of physical space, architects are consistently charged with creating spaces that will support the future. For the firm of Shepley Bulfinch Richardson & Abbott, involvement in the design of information commons began in 1988, with the Gateway Commons at Leavey Library, University of Southern California. Continuing through to our most recent projects, our designs have been driven by the goals and needs of those who teach, work, and study in these facilities. The focus of our design approach has been on accommodating changes to the physical environment in response to the evolution of a technological culture on the college campus. Our charge has been to create environments that provide long-term flexibility and act as catalysts in breaking down barriers to how students work and learn.

The commons as a concept originated as much from the need to provide integrated functionality in a technological learning environment as it did from a desire to improve unpleasant, claustrophobic, and unattractive computing centers and run-down library facilities that exist on many campuses. Once computing technology reached a basic saturation level on campus, designers and academic leaders began to think differently about space. Understanding how we work, how we learn, and what we need to be productive has launched planners and designers on an exploratory journey through contemporary shifts in and creative responses to the design of learning environments.

Throughout our involvement, we have encountered these broad, recurring themes:

- planning for flexibility: creating physical space solutions that enable change;
- designing for today's service models: reinforcing library and technology organizational models through the physical design of service points;
- customizing the information commons: developing unique design solutions in response to the specific needs of an institution;
- increasing breadth and complexity: providing a broader range of resources and services to support campus and community.

Although manifested differently for each institution, responses to these themes as a whole have shaped the programming, planning, and design of physical space. For both architects and institutions, the critical issue remains: what types of physical environments most successfully support learning in today's academic setting? This chapter presents the issues inherent in the physical design of commons and solutions for creating spaces that are attractive, supportive, and responsive to change, context, and community—places where teaching, research, and scholarship will flourish.

DESIGN FOR FLEXIBILITY

At many institutions, the process of achieving large-scale changes to the built environment does not keep pace with student expectations and needs. Too often, the evolution of curricula and research programs outpaces parallel changes in buildings and spaces. To compound the issue, student and faculty expectations are shaped by the faster rate of change seen in more nimble, market-driven commercial enterprises. To compete, the commons must be designed to be flexible and multiuse—a laboratory with multiple services where people come together to collaborate and learn.

The commons needs to include technology-rich, open areas that allow for reconfiguration and multiple simultaneous and consecutive uses. Change should not be limited to periodic renovations but should happen frequently over the course of a given day, month, or academic year. Weekday instructional spaces may become evening computer labs and Friday-night gaming parlors. The space can be thought of as an "academic loft" designed to change with us, not just remain a snapshot of space that is right for a fixed moment in time. Movable furniture, flexible panels, mobile white boards, and display surfaces can be utilized to define areas within a larger space. Wireless networks, prolific access to power and data connectivity and technological tools, nondirectional lighting and effective acoustics can create a flexible spatial armature that is engaging, inviting, and suitable for a variety of campus uses including library and IT services, instruction, and collaborative and informal learning activities—all of which entice the community to gather and create.

The need for flexibility has brought to the forefront design and technology tools for easily modifying an environment. A wall-sized projection area or digital screen allows for varied exchanges of information, imagery, and ideas at a pace that cannot be accommodated by static signage and displays. A room enclosed in glass allows visual connections to surrounding spaces, thus facilitating ease of access and supervision of multiple functions. When equipped with up-to-date technology tools, the room's functionality can be extended to include many types of use, including group study, video conferencing, consultation, and media viewing/editing. New library and office system furnishings are designed to allow both groups and individuals to work effectively. Chairs and tables come equipped with casters for easy relocation. Dividers that expand, contract, and roll from place to place allow groups to frequently reconfigure work and teaching space. The atmosphere of these spaces is charged with a design palette of vibrant color and texture, a change from institutional environments that have too often been bland and generic. We see these new tools and design strategies as a way forward to the realization of attractive, beautifully designed, flexible learning environments.

A primary factor driving the need for flexibility in the design of the commons has been the need to accommodate increasingly rapid shifts in users' behaviors and perceptions of format, media, and service. Continual shifts in information formats require the creation of space to house and enable the use of collections and tools that will change significantly over the life of the facility. Our increasingly visual culture, invigorated by the power of communicating through imagery and sound, is pushing information commons to meet an exploding need for access to multimedia resources. The physical space implications of accommodating this technology include digital labs with more and larger computer workstations for more sophisticated equipment and larger screens. The messy reality of producing the physical end-product generated in a sleek digital lab includes the need for graphic production work areas designed to hold large-format printers, bulky rolls of paper, and layout tables for working with poster-sized materials. Small, multiuse, enclosed rooms are needed for some media production and viewing functions, and storage, display, and tracking of media collections housed within the commons imply the use of shelving, accessories, and equipment that are more common in retail environments than traditional library and academic spaces.

In its Gottesman Libraries, Columbia University's Teachers College is planning two floors of reconfigurable space for use as digital research and production studios to support curricula and software development, scholarly publications, student and faculty research projects, lectures, forums, classes, and events. In these studios and labs, students and faculty will be able to work independently or together in open workstations and multiuse enclosed rooms that are suitable for small seminars, project work, video conferencing, and technology-rich media presentations. Plans include a raised floor system and suspended ceiling trellises to provide the infrastructure to support and distribute frequently changed wiring, lighting, and audiovisual equipment. Furniture and equipment storage rooms and a food-prep pantry will support transformation of the floors from digital workplace to event space. A lobby and digital display area at the entrance to each floor will be the fixed components that help orient and direct visitors to the more flexible studio space. Likewise, to anchor one end of the largest open work area, plans include a common gathering place where users will come together to discuss projects and ideas.

DESIGN FOR NEW SERVICE MODELS

Academic activity today is a multifaceted stream of gathering, thinking, exploring, and developing: more like a woven fabric or web than a linear use of resources. Immediacy of need is part of this way of working, and it is readily apparent in today's research environment. The implications of time on the ways in which service is provided need to be recognized as a critical aspect in the design of a commons, including enabling immediate access to tools, resources, and help.

Expectations for immediate access to services, together with tighter budgets and the demand for longer hours, have necessitated the promotion of self-service as a model throughout consumer-driven American culture. According to our surveys of student preferences in connection with the design of library and learning facilities, incoming student populations are accustomed to—and sometimes even prefer—do-it-yourself systems for understanding what is available and for accessing resources and information. The use of self-service can be leveraged to allow the commons to focus on person-to-person interaction for those activities in which it truly adds value, and student comfort with self-service models needs to be recognized in the location and configuration of service points.

At Lake Forest College's Donnelly and Lee Library, the commons is served from a single "one-stop shopping" service point that provides access services, research assistance, and computer help. The desk is positioned at one side of the commons' main thoroughfare, where it is easily visible, but not an obstacle to "do-it-yourself" visitors who wish to explore the commons on their own or visitors who are simply passing through the library on their way across campus. The desk is supplemented with self-service checkout machines and stand-up computer stations that provide efficient access to resources for the frequent, self-sufficient user.

An understanding of the specific service and work patterns of user populations will allow service points within the commons to be appropriately located and configured with visibility and efficiency in mind. Physical configurations designed to convey patterns of access and inquiry in a complex service environment, coupled with operational strategies, such as providing a single access point for all library and technology services or moving research and technology assistance out from behind a service desk, need to be clearly articulated so that they can inform the design of the physical space. Service desk design and the location of staff offices to support a "greeter" model, where initial contact is with a staff member whose role is to convey the range of services that are available, will differ from service points and staff areas designed to support sophisticated research help and in-depth assistance in the forming of questions.

The service desk in the commons at Marquette University's John P. Raynor Library accommodates both short-term and long-term assistance through its configuration. The relatively large desk is composed of several smaller-sized components to increase its approachability for users who need assistance. By breaking the desk down into several discrete components, there is room for patrons to linger for in-depth discussions with commons staff in one area while quick help with more routine needs continues nearby.

The commons challenges designers and institutions to identify new ways of organizing space and operations that reflect the changes brought on by the integration and convergence of resources and information formats in our technological society. Understanding this dynamic organization of services within the commons, including the extent of self-service activities, in-depth assistance, and converging staff roles and expertise, is essential in locating and configuring service points that are truly effective contributors to research and learning within the commons.

CUSTOMIZING THE INFORMATION COMMONS

The design of the commons should be approached within the context of a facility's or institution's unique characteristics. Like every other aspect of the campus, the commons must reinforce the unique needs of the students, the faculty, and the institution. Organizational and operational structures, space and funding parameters, and physical location all help shape an institution-specific design response to the "information commons" model.

An institution's organizational structure and affinities between the commons and other campus programs affect what is provided in the commons and how it is ordered. Partnerships to integrate the commons with other components of the library or other campus instructional and technology centers vary and ultimately affect the commons' program, budget, schedule, and physical design. Questions that institutions, planners, and designers must clarify in order to program and design the commons include:

- What are the specific operational and philosophical linkages between the library, IT, the student center, and various academic departments and professional schools?
- What resources and services are needed to support faculty curricular goals and pedagogical style?
- How are programs and facilities, such as writing centers, math labs, instructional spaces, tutoring, and honors programs, functionally supported within the commons?
- How do functions included in the commons interface with specialized information services and resources located elsewhere in the library and throughout the institution?

The institution's responses to these questions will clarify a philosophical framework for usage of the commons and prioritizations for usage of its physical space. Planners and designers can then organize functions accordingly—in strata that reflect their importance, level of activity, service requirements, and frequency of use. They can design the facility so that its entrance locations leverage access to important functions and so campus circulation routes through the commons connect it with other social and intellectual centers on campus. By creating design solutions that respond specifically to an institution's organizational structure and scale, programmatic priorities and synergies, and realities of budget and location, planners and designers contribute to the essential strength of the commons as an evolving tool that responds to an institution's style and patterns for learning, teaching, and working.

The physical size of the campus and the population it serves will ultimately influence the scale and character of the commons. At Indiana University, Bloomington, the large size of the campus and the distance students must travel between classes and home increase their reliance on the library's information commons as a place to study between classes. In addition to providing a café, help services for computer and reference requests, and instructional spaces to support information literacy, the information commons in the Herman B. Wells Library has responded to this specific need by providing an open, flexible space on the main entrance level of the library with over 350 computers for student use. At Elon University, which serves a much smaller campus population, the look and feel of the commons in the Carol Grotnes Belk Library emphasizes small-scale settings where—reinforcing the university's curricular goals—students can receive personalized attention and academic support. The inclusion of social space, such as a café, within the Belk Library was less of a priority because of its location adjacent to the university's campus center.

Occasionally the opportunity arises to create a new information commons that, by location, changes the way in which an academic community interacts. More often, the location of the information commons is predetermined by the form of the existing library or other facility in which it will be located. In either situation, the facility's location will affect the types of programs offered and the ways in which services and resources are arrayed within the commons. For instance, the Robert W. Woodruff Library at Emory University is located at the edge of the main campus, where it helps to define one boundary of the academic district. Its commons is a destination point for patrons who seek critical resources and services, much like an anchor store in a shopping district. The commons area in the Donnelley and Lee Library at Lake Forest College is designed as a physical link that unites academic and residential areas of campus. At Dartmouth College, the "Street of Services" runs the length of the Baker-Berry Library and draws people through the facility as they move from one side of campus to the other.

When the information commons becomes a crossroads with multiple entrances, it is necessary to think differently about security and to seek design solutions that meet this need without creating barriers to the way people want to move and work. As more information is available in digital form, libraries' concern for the security of print material will evolve, so that the book security system and the building perimeter may not be one and the same. New approaches to collection security, bolstered by the advent of new technologies and systems that change operational procedures and improve collection organization and coherence, will also help lessen dependence on rigid security systems that are obstacles to users.

Dynamic spatial and programmatic concepts that contribute to the vitality and strength of the commons facility can be the result of facing budgetary realities and space constraints. In planning the commons, the campus should be viewed as a whole in order to emphasize shared uses and to minimize redundant space. An institution may be attracted to the commons' ability to combine classrooms, food venues, and multiuse event spaces with more traditional library and technology program components in order to create a single, strong facility that is open longer hours. At the 5,000-student College of Saint Catherine, in St. Paul, Minnesota, the library, information technology services, academic support, student center, dining hall, and chapel are all interconnected in the Coeur de Catherine, thus creating a learning commons that encompasses social, intellectual, and spiritual growth.

When funding a large project is not feasible, institutions may approach the information commons as a smaller place for experimentation with new services and resources. In the design of a small, experimental commons, with a lower cost and less investment of physical space, institutions can more easily afford risk-taking with programs and design. Rice University's Electronic Resources Center, an open-plan learning lab with flexible settings for group and individual work, was implemented in an area that became available when the business school re-located to a new building. In this space, both the physical and operational aspects of an open, collaborative environment were tested and refined to inform a subsequent, larger renovation within the main Fondren Library. In Wellesley College's Clapp Library, the Knapp Center was created from an underutilized basement area by transforming a relic lounge space for student gatherings in the 1960s into a leading-edge media and technology center. The success of the Knapp Center has led to further integration of digital resources and tools in subsequent renovations of other areas of the library.

These examples are representative of the breadth of design possibilities inherent in the commons model. In each instance, the success of the facility depends on customization of the design and program to address unique institutional parameters such as scale, budget, location, and programmatic priorities. The strength of the information commons model as a spatial and functional reality lies in its adaptability to the specific identity of campus learning culture.

INCREASING BREADTH AND COMPLEXITY

The commons continues to thrive by evolving to support new ways of working. Commons spaces now include broad and complex arrays of services that reach far beyond the integration of library and IT tools that were originally the genesis of the information commons. Commons today may include writing centers, math labs, media production studios, experimental classrooms, digital content development facilities, video conferencing, and large-format printing areas. The iPod phenomenon extends the physical boundaries of learning even further, and student laptops now function as mobile, personalized media centers through iTunes, iMovie, DVD players, instant messaging, and software for writing, drawing, editing, and collaborating.

An ongoing challenge that affects the commons design is the need for institutions to creatively connect a broader cross section of the campus community, particularly faculty, with the happenings of the commons. This has led to the incorporation of a greater range of space uses, including event spaces, experimental classrooms, exhibit areas, curriculum development labs, and academic support services. With these new components and activities, boundaries between library/learning center and campus/community center have begun to blur, and the commons concept has gradually transitioned from early library- and computing-focused information commons to a more inclusive model, the academic commons.

With this increased breadth of services, the commons becomes a place to showcase the campus community and activities of many types. Accordingly, its spaces must be transformable for "instant theater": parties, conferences, forums, and events. With expanded usage, a host of new design and operational challenges emerge: access for larger volumes of people, increased maintenance, parking, and more complex zoning of physical space. With these challenges come opportunities to capitalize on the excitement created by expanded ranges of activity that attract attention and draw in the community. Most importantly, these new uses enhance the richness and vitality of the commons. People want to study, work, socialize, and attend events in a place that is majestic, innovative, "cool," or memorable. Vibrant colors, textures, and materials, and attractive, comfortable furnishings give identity to the facility and create an intellectual and social learning environment that is met with delight from its users.

The blossoming of the information commons, from its initial conception as an integrated access point for technology tools, and print and electronic information resources into a dynamic organization for the support of teaching, learning, information literacy, social intellectual engagement, and student and faculty excellence, is evidenced by tracing the physical form of these facilities over the past two decades.

The first information commons project with which Shepley Bulfinch was involved was the Gateway Commons at the Leavey Library, University of Southern California. An early model for subsequent commons, it was developed in 1988, when the growing importance of computing to academic research necessitated the rethinking of physical space at USC. Its program components and synergies were to become hallmarks of the space type: a learning place within the library where students could use computers to access electronic information resources in tandem with use of the library's print reference collections, nearby electronic classrooms, open computer workstations to support collaborative work, and glass-enclosed group study rooms. In the subsequent creation of a vision for the Baker-Berry Library at Dartmouth College, in 1996, the program components of the Leavey Library information commons were built upon to create a commons-type learning environment that integrates media and digital production services and includes a 24/7 café that provides a place for intellectual conversation and connection to community news and events. Its physical organization was designed to be more inclusive: its "street of services" runs through the entire library to connect reference, circulation, computing help, academic computing professionals, reference librarians, a computer store, the café, and the media center. Today, developers of commons projects continue to seek expansion in the breadth of services provided. Georgia Tech is planning the integration of their library and Undergraduate Learning Center to create a new complex that emphasizes support of the undergraduate educational experience. The facility will contain transformable spaces suitable for performances, exhibits, and experiential learning, and will include work areas for academic advising, international education, and other student success programs. Other institutions have similar facilities in the planning stages, each of which provides a unique array of resources appropriate to its institution's academic mission and vision. Most are depending on technologically robust, reconfigurable, multiuse space designs to achieve their goals.

CONCLUSION

The information commons has expanded far beyond its genesis in library and IT environments, and has come into its own. It is a distinct type of learning space that accommodates change. Its shape is unique to an institution's culture and population and brings together the best of campus learning resources. Planned to leverage the efficiency of reconfigurable and multiuse areas, its physical form provides fluid connections between varied activity zones, addresses acoustical control within open and enclosed areas, and accommodates increasingly robust infusions of technology tools and infrastructure. The environment is enhanced by palettes of rich colors and textures that provide a vibrant look and feel, and by the use of glass and open space to provide transparency and visual connection. Taken together, these physical characteristics define a new academic space type whose genesis was the information commons.

During the early planning phases for learning environments such as commons, we have heard from countless student groups about the operational quirks of campuses that were not planned to include current technology tools and curricular approaches: running back and forth between the library and the computing lab, standing in line for a space in the lab, having to pack up and leave to take a study break or get something to eat, and the lack of places to work together on campus, even though classes require more and more group work. Learning spaces best address these problems if they are approached as user-driven environments where students and faculty are the designers of the way they want to work: with tools, resources, and each other. The development of user-driven design responses is the most important aspect of any commons project. The more we explore how people are actually working with new and diverse tools, the better we can anticipate their needs. As a design strategy, this will allow the information commons to meet the future and make the most of it, to focus on discovery, and to leave barriers behind.

4

Technology in the Information Commons

Richard Bussell,
Vantage Technology Consulting Group

M ost librarians and library planners agree that the future of the library is intimately associated with technology, but many of them also harbor a concern that digital access to information will make the physical library—with its traditional print collection and helpful, knowledgeable, and supportive staff—irrelevant to students and faculty.

At the same time, proponents of technology in the library argue that embracing technology and planning for a new or revitalized library based around a technology-rich information commons is the very thing that will draw students into the library more frequently, and will reinforce the library's role at the center of academic pursuits and campus life. The information commons enhances the library by centralizing and consolidating technology functions, facilities, and systems aimed squarely at information access, academic research, and teaching and learning.

This chapter offers a conceptual overview of an information commons of the future. It examines a series of technology-driven components, all of which could be accomplished in some form today, and discusses each component's relevance and application in the context of the library.

INTEGRATING TECHNOLOGY INTO PLACE AND PURPOSE

Technology is certainly not alien to the library. In the past twenty years, many technology-based components have been added to traditional library functions: sophisticated portal-based access to online information, computer labs, large format scanners and printers, graphics editing software, file format conversion, CD and DVD burning, and a host of other functions.

But libraries have not always *integrated* technology naturally into their spaces or their purposes. They may have computers and perhaps an area labeled "Information Commons," but in reality these spaces are often little more than computer labs that happen to be located in the library (and frequently in the basement!). In some cases, there are fundamental divisions between the computer lab and the library, which are created and reinforced by funding, development, management, and support arrangements that are provided by different campus groups. Such arrangements, though they may place technology in the library, perpetuate a notion of the library as separate from these tools and the roles they play in teaching and learning.

The information commons, when realized as an integrated learning environment, has the potential to connect disparate components and to exploit that connection to reinforce the library's position at the center of academic research, teaching, and learning. The information commons is a place where students and faculty come to *use* both technology and traditional materials, to *learn* how to use technology effectively in their academic pursuits, and to *discover* new (and potentially disruptive) educational technologies alongside those with which they are already comfortable. (Exposure to disruptive technologies potentially enables users to leapfrog established ideas or to consider previously inconceivable approaches to a task.) An "open computing environment" (described in more detail below) resides at the center of the information commons and provides consolidated access to information, tools, and library services.

The proximity of components, the encouragement to experiment with new technologies and new resources, and the active participation of library staff who are knowledgeable in the concurrent use of the traditional resources, conventional technologies, and potentially disruptive new technologies—all in pursuit of teaching, learning, and research—are key factors in realizing an effective information commons.

The following sections describe how the components of an imaginary information commons enhance the role of the library on campus. These scenarios proceed from the traditional or commonplace to the unconventional. Though futuristic in focus, many of these scenarios could be enacted today, using existing technologies to support habits of research, teaching, and learning at an institution.

Connect Print Collections and Computers

In the cutting-edge information commons, the print collection remains a fundamental resource (albeit one of many). Frequently accessed books are located adjacent to, and easily accessible from, the open computing environment and other information commons components in order to facilitate and encourage multimodal research. In some institutions, the overall size of the collection available on open shelving may be reduced, with less-frequently requested volumes housed in an automatic storage and retrieval system (ASRS) or an off-site repository. To provide immediate access to the text collection, excerpts from books (perhaps sample chapters) are available for browsing online, and reading these excerpts often prompts students to seek out the books in their entirety. Students and researchers are encouraged to relocate books to a temporary personal collection near their study area. Unique radio frequency identification (RFID) tags enable the library staff to locate these books for later reshelving, or when urgently requested by other patrons.

Consolidate Online Access to Information

Access to citation and full-text databases, online journals, and electronic collections in the larger library consortium are available through a secure portal, with restricted access to special materials based on their course enrollment and registered research interests. The portal integrates library materials with online learning tools, and is available through a browser on any computer with local or remote access to the campus network.

Accommodate Social Learning in an Open Computing Environment

The open computing environment is far from the quiet study space of the traditional library. It has more in common with the environment in a lively office bullpen or a busy coffee shop, where important work takes place in a collaborative manner amid a bustle of activity. There are no individual study carrels in this environment. Instead, groups of students sit in close proximity and in full view of each other. As in office workstations, each student work area is arranged with space for books, papers, and a visitor chair alongside the computer. Students focus their attention on (or divide their attention between, depending on your point of view!) studies and socializing, and both activities occur in multiple windows on a large, double-width, touch-sensitive flat panel screen located at each seat. The screen displays office applications, multiple course work and research portals, personal websites, instant messaging windows, and multiple audio and video feeds that display material from campus content servers and from the Internet. The computers are loaded with collaborative browsing software that enables students to share information as they view it. This shared view includes classmates sitting on the other side of the information commons or on the other side of campus—or on the other side of the world! Most workstations are configured with a full PC or Mac, but some have no visible processor. These workstations provide large screens and keyboards for direct connection to students' laptops, PDAs (personal digital assistants), or UMPCs (ultra mobile PCs). Every seat has desktop connections for USB and Firewire-equipped personal storage devices. Walk-up PCs, intended for short-term browsing and information access, are available and will remain in operation at least until personal mobile devices can provide a graphics experience comparable to a desktop LCD monitor.

In addition to single-person workstations, there are small-group areas outfitted with a collaborative application server using software like TeamSpot. Individual students in the group use their own laptops to seamlessly contribute material to a team project that is hosted on the server and displayed on a large, high-resolution screen.

Flat-panel monitors, mounted on perimeter walls and suspended from the ceiling throughout the information commons, contribute to the overall ambience and energy level in the space. The screens display information from a coordinated digital signage and video distribution system that delivers a mix of campus news and information, campus "branding" and material related to current campus activities, information encouraging participation in current activities in the information commons, student-generated video and graphics material, and live television news feeds and special events. The audio from every program (and a channel selector) is available simultaneously at each seat as subtitles and as a headphone feed.

Support Wireless Network Connectivity

Gigabit campus network connectivity is provided in the open computing environment and in other areas with high bandwidth requirements. In addition, the entire information commons includes a shared internal antenna to support ubiquitous wireless networking. The antenna, integrated into the fabric of the building during facility design, ensures high wireless network signal strength. The system supports access to multiple wireless services including wireless access to the campus data network using the 802.11 (Wi-Fi) and 802.16 (WiMAX) protocols. It also carries EV-DO (Evolution-Data Optimized) and HSPDA (High Speed Data Packet Access) wireless radio broadband connections provided by cellular carriers. As a result, faculty and students can reliably access and download material that they previously researched, created, or stored using their personal portable devices, irrespective of the network path or provider they choose.

Provide More Advanced Technology Training

In the information commons, faculty and students discover new technologies and, with support from the library staff, learn how to use these new tools effectively. This process includes both formal training sessions and informal one-on-one and small-group support. Most libraries have been involved in training students to use technology-enabled search methods since the early years of online databases. Over time, that role expanded to include formal training in basic computer literacy. Students from many departments attend classes in the library to learn the basics of Word, Excel, and other basic office productivity programs. In the future, students will need greater competency with advanced software and technology tools in order to complete their course assignments. Contrary to popular perceptions, many students today need extensive training to assimilate the necessary academic technology skills.

In the not-too-distant future, the information commons will become the campus's training center in a range of technological subjects and skills, including

- general computer literacy;
- making presentations using presentation software and the web;
- creating graphics, animation, and video;

- visual modeling and using visualization resources;
- database applications in simulation and use of simulation resources.

Support Instruction through Faculty Production Labs

Campus groups concerned with pedagogy and teaching methods are compelled to consider and advise faculty on the impact and effectiveness of new technologies. On many campuses, the learning support groups who are concerned with pedagogical strategies for developing skills and teaching concepts are separate from the groups with expertise in procuring, deploying, and operating classroom technologies. The information commons provides an opportunity to co-locate these groups and to consolidate campus knowledge and experience in course redesign and effective use of instructional technology, to produce engaging course content and collaborative study models that enhance educational outcomes.

The faculty production lab provides tools and support necessary for faculty to develop and produce course material. The lab includes PC or Mac workstations with large-screen monitors, loaded with the software and tools required to produce high-quality presentations, graphics, animation, video, and visualization materials. Selected peripheral equipment is also available to enhance production quality—key to capturing and holding student attention! A small video recording area (an open studio) may also be part of the faculty production lab. This studio will include digital video cameras, studio lighting, cyclorama, and green screen for live video recording of "talking heads" and small demonstrations. The faculty production lab is closely coupled with an experimental technology classroom (described in the next section) for demonstrating and developing course material using advanced and experimental technology.

Enhance Production Values in Student Media Production

For more than fifteen years, since PCs became an accepted part of libraries, students have expected libraries to provide access to technology that is beyond their individual means. Currently students look to the library for equipment and assistance when they have a need to produce high-quality video. Today's high-end PCs and Macs are quite capable of handling video production, but until such equipment becomes commonplace and affordable, the information commons will continue to provide a center for student media and video production. Staff in the lab or located immediately adjacent provide support to help students extract maximum academic benefit from the facilities.

The student media production lab is similar to the open computing lab environment, but is based on newer and more advanced PC and Mac workstations (those using the latest dual-core and twin dual-core processors), multiple widescreen monitors, and industry standard audio and video software. Peripherals provide easy ingestion of video from analog and digital formats, support creative and tactile editing, and provide for publishing directly to DVD and the Internet. A small video recording area is provided or may be shared with the faculty production lab (details above).

Encourage Experimentation with New Instructional Technology

New instructional technology for the classroom is caught in a "catch-22" situation. It is not possible to justify spending money on new classroom technologies until proven worthwhile, and it is not possible to teach—and thus demonstrate that new technologies are relevant and worthwhile—until they are installed in classrooms. One possible solution to this dilemma is to develop and fund an experimental technology classroom.

Experimental technology classrooms incorporate technologies not available in standard smart classrooms. They enable faculty to evaluate new technologies in real classroom situations and to teach classes using media-rich course content, interactive techniques, and technology-enhanced active learning that they developed in the faculty production lab. Successful technologies—those that are pedagogically effective and popular with faculty—will be rolled out to some or all campus classrooms.

The technologies installed in the experimental room at any one time will be highly dependent on the campus curriculum and pedagogical style. Currently many institutions are holding focus groups and workshop discussions to allow faculty to voice opinions on classroom technology and pedagogy. The following ideas summarize a series of concepts discussed in those workshops:

- A hybrid lecture/lab classroom: a room configured as a hybrid lecture room/ collaborative student computer lab that will enable lecture and technology-enhanced active learning formats to be combined in a single class period. New technology-specific furniture systems are emerging to support concepts like this.
- Enhanced and more flexible presentation capabilities: a room with presentation technologies, including real-time annotation of course materials and random access to resource materials, that will reduce dependence on prepared presentations and allow faculty to develop material in response to class discussion.
- Student response and collaboration technologies: a room that uses technology to encourage students to respond and engage using clicker or PDA feedback devices. More sophisticated versions allow faculty members to accept output from multiple student computers for display on the main screen via a wireless network connection.
- Lecture recording and review technologies: a room equipped with technology for capturing and recording audiovisual presentation material. Because education continues to move toward a participatory format, students must be able to accurately reconstruct the manner in which a solution was developed during class. As a result, many campuses are experimenting with automated classroom video capture and replay-on-demand.

The design of experimental technology classrooms should encourage regular technology refresh because "static" rooms, however much in demand by faculty and students, will lose their reason for being: experimental classrooms *must* continually *evolve* to help position their institutions at the forefront of effective classroom technology.

Challenge Existing Uses of Technology

Libraries have traditionally provided educational resources that are beyond the reach of individual students, and advanced technology labs continue and extend that tradition. They go above and beyond mainstream technologies that are by now expected in the library, and introduce unexpected and potentially disruptive technologies that users would not otherwise encounter. Whereas a user may go to the library to seek out technologies he understands and needs, advanced technology labs present technologies that he has never considered using. Advanced technology labs seek out technologies that are narrowly defined as research tools—and therefore confined to individual schools or departments—but which have the potential to become everyday tools with much wider application. Straightforward technology transfer between disciplines often produces rapid and spectacular results, and students find uses for technology that the original creators never envisioned. Advanced technology labs enable these quantum leaps by publicizing technologies to diverse groups of users, providing early and open access, and providing knowledgeable and creative support staff. Advanced technology labs will move libraries closer to research groups on campus and may even become campus centers for exploring cross-disciplinary application of technology.

Current technologies that might be offered in the advanced technology lab include

- animation and graphics software, data visualization software, and advanced graphics tablets, for producing and interacting visually with a wide range of data;
- application development and database environments, for moving beyond spreadsheet analysis to develop simulation tools; and
- 3-D modeling tools and 3-D printers/rapid prototyping machines, for realizing solid forms in engineering, architectural, and artistic endeavors.

Access Campus and Global Simulation and Visualization Resources

Simulation and visualization are already playing an important role in research, and will play an increasingly important role in teaching and learning. Simulation involves modeling natural systems or human systems in the computer to gain insight into their functions and to show the effects of alternative conditions and constraints. Visualization is concerned with the presentation of interactive or animated digital images to users as an aid to understanding data. For example, scientists "visualize" huge quantities of laboratory, field, or simulation data as an aid to reasoning and understanding.

Simulation and visualization are in use in nearly all subject areas, including the sciences, mathematics and computing, geography, history, human behavior, and business. Students from all disciplines who are exposed to simulation and visualization technologies in the classroom will want to access, review, and work with these tools in their own time to contrast and compare similar tools developed in other departments and institutions. Students will want to investigate and understand the benefits and limitations of alternative approaches, the use of simplifying approximations and assumptions, and the fidelity and validity of the simulation outcomes. Libraries are natural places for students to look for the technology, resources, and support necessary to accomplish these tasks.

In medical education, where simulation techniques are already in frequent use, schools are planning information commons that will combine print collections, physical and virtual simulation, and visualization resources for students' use. Many simulations in medical education combine both physical and virtual simulation components. They involve a plastic simulation of the relevant anatomy linked to a computer that is programmed to respond to the students' input in a variety of real life reactions. In other medical simulations, visualizations are accomplished using 3-D CT or MRI scans, and haptic interfaces provide physical feedback in response to users' actions.

On a larger scale, and with a longer-term view, information commons will become the natural place students look to for technology and knowledge necessary to access and utilize global simulation and research resources. For instance, researchers around the globe can access "Earth Simulator," a supercomputer located in Japan that runs global climate models and evaluates the effects of global warming using holistic simulations of the global climate in both the atmosphere and the oceans.

CONCLUSION

Today's information commons represent a snapshot in the evolution of libraries and their inevitable ongoing relationship with technology. Libraries will undoubtedly continue their long tradition of dedicated support to teaching, learning, and discovery. Many libraries are already embracing technology, integrating it with the core of their mission, and creating information commons aimed squarely at academic research, teaching, and learning. Students and faculty come to an information commons to *use* both technology and traditional materials, to *learn* how to use technology effectively in their academic pursuits, and to *discover* new educational technologies. In addition, faculty will recognize information commons as centers for best practice in effective use of educational technologies, and they will use the facilities to *develop* new course content and to *teach classes* using promising emerging technologies not available elsewhere on campus.

Information commons will provide access to tools and resources that are out of reach of the average student, and will continually upgrade available mainstream technologies and introduce emerging and potentially disruptive technologies that would otherwise be narrowly defined as specialized research tools. For example, information commons will naturally evolve to support faculty and student inquiries into simulation and visualization techniques and technologies as they evolve from pure research tools to assume a place in everyday teaching, learning, and discovery.

Information commons, as such, are difficult to define. The "information commons" isn't found in any one system, facility, support group, or technology, but rather, in the convergence of many component parts that are co-located in a welcoming and open facility. Perhaps even more fundamental to the definition is the notion of continual change; next year's information commons will have evolved to incorporate new emerging needs, ensuring that the information commons remains a continuously moving target.

5

———◆———

Case Study in Customizing Information Commons Environments: Hardin Library

James Duncan, Colorado State Library

Libraries seeking to recast their role as vibrant service centers, capable of responding to or even forecasting the needs of their user communities, are repurposing their physical spaces and developing new services. The past decade has been an exciting and challenging time, providing opportunity for many libraries and creating angst for others.

As a general model, an information commons provides a tangible intersection for information-rich delivery services, self-paced learning or research, and user-driven digital-content creation activities. Beyond these core offerings, however, most libraries with a desire to serve the specialized needs of their particular communities are looking for ways to tweak the model.

This chapter will discuss two types of customization—physical space enhancements and new-breed services. While practical lessons will be highlighted from the Information Commons at the University of Iowa's Hardin Library for the Health Sciences, several general themes will emerge that can guide any institution seeking to customize learning spaces and services. The most important lesson: customization is enormously dependent on a deep understanding of the library's client community.

CASE STUDY BACKGROUND

The Information Commons at Hardin Library is an example of how to successfully customize a facility's physical learning environment and its service offerings for a particular user population. Constructed in 1996 and doubled in size in 1999, the Information Commons continues to serve as a central support and delivery venue for multimedia courseware, hands-on classroom instruction, and independent learning. It boasts several high-end multimedia development workstations, two fifty-seat electronic classrooms, and information research workstations for searching health-related databases and the Internet, as well as for word processing, e-mail, and other productivity applications.

While modeled in part from the Information Arcade located in the Main Library[1] of the University of Iowa, the Information Commons at Hardin Library developed in very different ways to address the needs of the academic health science user populations it serves. Faculty members from the College of Public Health, for instance, have very different needs than dental students. Nursing students have different needs than biomedical researchers. Based in the library and managed by librarians, the Commons offered a user-focused support structure and was responsive to emerging technology needs.

The success of a facility like the Information Commons, however, is not achieved without collaboration and ongoing support from stakeholder partners. At Hardin Library, three discrete and separate IT organizations contributed to the technology support behind the facility, its electronic classrooms, its open-access stations, and its services.

REQUIRED: A CHAMPION FOR THE CAUSE

Collaboration does not just "happen." Collaboration requires a champion or an evangelist, someone willing to take responsibility for brokering relationships, casting a vision, or shaping the direction for the initiative. Inviting stakeholders to the "sandbox," sharing space and toys, can be fun—but is not always fun and games. Collaboration is hard work, but enormously gratifying for all involved when it succeeds. Still, at least one person must serve in the role.

During the first three years of operations for the Information Commons at Hardin Library, the College of Medicine's IT department contributed half of a desktop support position to help install, configure, and troubleshoot computers. Infrastructure support was offered through access to file servers and application servers. None of this support was offered simply on the basis of goodwill, but rather with an understanding from the outset that the library and this stakeholder IT department were trying to serve the *same population* of users in the most effective way. The basis for collaboration was the identification of a *common service goal*. The college had contributed financially to the construction of the facility's electronic classroom, and so had a stake in seeing the facility succeed. The library had contributed space and staffing, and was on a mission to establish a service focused on the teaching and learning needs of the health colleges. Both entities wished to see the facility impact its users in innovative and nontraditional ways.

The champion's role at Hardin Library was to remind both the library and its partners, in an ongoing diplomatic and open manner, of this common service goal—not once, not for a few months, but consistently over the course of several years.

EVOLUTION OF THE COMMONS

From the opening of its doors, the facility was overrun. After two years of success-ful operations (and documented heavy patron traffic), planning for an expanded Commons began. An opportunity for collaboration again emerged. For several years, a typical "ITC," or computer lab, had been operating in the lower level of the library. This lab was like any other standard student computer lab on campus, with virtually no relationship to the collections or services of the library. This lab was administrated by a central IT department, with support offices located on the other side of campus. User support was provided by computer science and engi-neering undergraduate students who, though technically capable, had not been hired with public service skills as a core competency. Some of them, for whom English was not their native language, struggled with communication.

Meanwhile, one floor above, the Information Commons had been constructed as a community-focused learning-resource center. Comfortable spaces for indi-vidual and group activities provided an environment more appealing to many students. A three-tier support system had been created in the Commons, with service-oriented undergraduate students serving as the front-line desk staff. Graduate assistants, who coupled expertise in multimedia production with its application to teaching and learning, served as backup. Full-time professional library staff provided a unique combination of support at the top tier, drawing together traditional information research skills, an understanding of scholarly publishing trends, and interest in exploring the impacts for new technologies on higher education.

Essentially, a dichotomy in service had been created within the library. Imag-ine patrons' confusion: in the same building, two "computing" facilities were available. Each location offered access to a different set of servers and software resources, and each facility was guided by different policies. Patrons who tried to pursue a mix of learning activities (checking e-mail, writing a paper, accessing a multimedia learning title on CD-ROM, utilizing a statistics program, scanning some images, creating a presentation, or any number of other tasks) found them-selves able to do some of their work in one location and *then having to pick up and move one floor* to the other location for the rest of their academic work.

Rather than continue this dichotomy of service between these separate areas (and asking patrons to understand the governance structure and departmental territories that had caused this establishment of separate but similar facilities), planners for the expansion of the Information Commons invited multiple IT staff and faculty stakeholders into the planning process. The group soon identified a strategy and solution: the ITC would move up one floor to merge with the Commons. The stated goal: students would be able to sit down to any computer anywhere on the floor and have access to whatever service or software title they wished to utilize. Staffing at the second service desk would be managed under the same three-tier, library-centric system already in place at the Commons.

By focusing on serving students' needs, the collaboration's champion success-fully brokered technical and governance solutions between the two IT stakehold-ers and the library. For several years, a visible testimonial to the endurance of the partnership could be seen on each desktop throughout the Commons—a custom wallpaper stated: "This facility supported by Healthcare Information Systems (HCIS), Information Technology Services (ITS) and Hardin Library for the Health Sciences." Students likely didn't understand the significance of the collaboration (nor did they care). The important impact: patrons could go about their academic work efficiently, with a minimum of confusion about where to access software, servers, and library resources.

CORE TO ANY COMMONS: COLLABORATION

During the past decade, many information commons–type facilities have been developed around the United States and abroad. In their own way, each is customized to the local environment in which they are constructed, and each is focused on serving a distinct population of patrons. The information commons is a pliable model that blends technology, reference, instruction, and integrated service. In academic libraries it might include a writing center or instructional support services for faculty members (like a center for teaching). In public libraries, it might feature a cybercafé or technology training area. In some of the most notable installations, it is apparent that despite their geographic or demographic or service differences, each incarnation of an information (learning; knowledge) commons shares a common trait—they are collaboratively planned, implemented, and supported by the library and at least one other stakeholder. The importance of collaboration cannot be underestimated, and it is crucial to invest real energy (not lip service) in building those relationships. True collaborative effort will guarantee success and ensure high impact for users, sustainability of resources, and ongoing advocacy for the library.

CUSTOMIZING PHYSICAL SPACES

Redesigning or retrofitting space for technology often proves tricky in libraries constructed before 1970 or even as late as 1980. A building's anatomy directly constrains the manner in which an information commons can be planned, designed, constructed, or customized for its user community. Think of architecture as bones, and preexisting infrastructure elements like electrical or telecommunication wiring as arteries, and one has some idea for the challenges involved with the rearrangement of a library's internal organs or the grafting of a new appendage. Such a procedure requires planning, staging, and the involvement of a surgical team of experts to include librarians, IT specialists, AV specialists, and most importantly, members of the directly affected user community.

Hardin Library was constructed between 1971 and 1973 and opened for users in 1974. Designed by Walter Netsch, of the Chicago architectural firm Skidmore, Owings and Merrill, the building's structure provided challenges. Hardin's architectural design is considered to be an example of Netsch's signature "Field Theory," a construct where basic squares are rotated into complex geometries. Fortunately, space designated for the Information Commons and its first electronic classroom featured a sizeable 5,000-square-foot area internal to the building, so the nonsquared angles that are a signature feature of the building's exterior were not a major barrier. However, given the age of the building, the area designated for the Commons lacked existing conduits for pulling electrical and network cabling. This is not surprising; personal computers and user-level network access to electronic journals and multimedia learning titles were hardly a glimmer on the horizon for libraries. These and other types of environmental constraints are typical for most libraries and simply must be factored into electronic classroom design in order to determine arrangements for powered/networked individual and group-learning spaces, and other user-production spaces.

Having learned some lessons from the 1992 construction of the Main Library Information Arcade, the planners for the 1995 to 1996 construction of the Hardin Library Information Commons (later named Information Commons East) focused on several enhancements to the preexisting model:

1. *Improving the flow of traffic and breaking away from the typical feel of an institutionalized "computer lab."* Open space through the entryway, with comfortable seating as a border, transitioned to functional areas that maintained a sense of openness. Indirect lighting, placed strategically, reduced glare on computer monitors and created a calm mood. Designers contributing to the project emphasized nonlinear details to contrast with the "impersonal" technologies deployed at each work space.

2. *Designing significantly more space between rows in the electronic classroom.* A common mistake in electronic classroom design is to pack as many computers as possible into a room, with a goal of maximizing the number of users in a teaching session. The result is poor learning space, which, ironically, can become underutilized. Attendees are cramped, air temperature frequently becomes an issue, and the instructor has little opportunity to move around the room. At Hardin Library, the initial 1,900-square-foot classroom space could have accommodated thirty-five or even forty computers. This would have resulted in cramped quarters and tight rows. The decision to limit to twenty-five computers (but retain seating for fifty) was wise; instructors and session attendees frequently commented about how spacious the classroom felt. That feedback was proof that properly designed space could eliminate one barrier for learning.

3. *Broadening the amount of desk surface space, including classroom work tables, to address the changing nature of student study behaviors.* This decision was fortuitous in that it not only addressed a desire to provide more usable space per square foot, but it allowed the Commons to better serve users who work together on projects or in study groups. Providing ample space facilitated collaboration activities. During nonscheduled hours, the classroom also became a place where users gravitated to work in groups.

4. *Providing dedicated access at three spots for laptop computer users to jack in to the campus network with convenient access to electrical outlets above the work surface.* Of the four planned enhancements, this one failed. A belief at the time was that users seeking high-speed network access would be desperate for places to connect. After two years of observing the laptop zone used only a handful of times, the area was converted to accommodate standard desktop comput-

ers. The problem with the laptop zone was that the design enhancement was planned based on *assumption* rather than actual *assessment* of user needs. In 1996, laptops were not nearly as common as they are today, and users were not as mobile as they are today. The technological factor responsible for the increased sales of laptops and the mobility of laptop users during the past ten years is obvious: wireless networking. Offering "untethered" access to the network does not obviate the need to enhance spaces for mobile users, but it does change how space is designed and how details are implemented.

EVOLVING SPACE:
CREATING FLEXIBILITY AND FUTURE POTENTIAL

Enhancement of physical learning spaces became an evolutionary process. Planners for the 1998 to 1999 expansion of the Information Commons West considered ways to better address the growing demand for small group-oriented spaces, collaborative spaces, and learner-centered classroom teaching. The results included:

1. *A flexible, reconfigurable, and divisible electronic classroom with simplified room controls.* With moveable tables and three options for layouts, the new classroom offered clusters of user workstations. Emphasis in the space was on small-group interaction and elimination of the traditional forward-facing, instructor-focused classroom layout typically found in such teaching spaces.
2. *Additional small-group work carrels.* Curricular trends that have changed the way users study and learn could be enhanced with spaces that comfortably accommodated two or three individuals and a computer.
3. *A small conference room suitable for eight to twelve individuals and openly available to faculty-led sessions or student-led study groups.* Facility planners observed and talked with instructors who utilized Commons spaces, and came to understand that in some cases, reserving an electronic classroom was considered overkill for a small group, particularly if hands-on access to computers for all participants wasn't a crucial part of the teaching/discussion session.

RECURRING INVESTMENT REQUIRED

Commitment to an information commons does not end with the last brush stroke of paint or the final deployment of a new computer. Ever-changing and new technologies certainly come to play in a deep way, introducing challenges to staffing roles and service impacts for information commons facilities. The advancement in collaborative technologies, audiovisual technologies, media formats, hardware and software, or other factors require that facilities be planned for future potential. Flexibility in design is crucial, and increasingly, users and instructors expect that physical learning spaces like an information commons should offer the latest technology resources.

For instance, in the late 1990s, users did not demand facilities (equipment, software, or studio spaces) for creating podcasts. In 2007, some users may be asking for those capabilities at their local information commons. Most users witness technologies in the entertainment and consumer world changing rapidly, and do not understand why libraries' physical facility budgets are not deep enough or flexible enough to match the pace of technology evolution. It is imperative that planners, administrators, and stakeholder partners identify sustainable models for infusing an information commons with new technology as well as human resources to support those tools.

WANT SUSTAINABILITY? COLLABORATE

A champion's work continues beyond the completion of learning space construction. That person must stay connected with the community of users, identify and respond nimbly to users' shifting information needs, and understand the content creation needs or learning needs of that user community. Most importantly, the champion for collaboration must continue to explore nontraditional partnerships and resource-sharing opportunities.

Clearly, sustainability is an ongoing challenge for any sector of a library's service offerings. However, with a well-established, tangible partnership underlying an information commons, the library does not have to address the challenge alone. In the case of Hardin Library's Commons, for instance, one core collaborator was a central IT department, the Campus Services division. This outside partner consistently committed hardware resources to benefit the greater good of the campus community. This department, as well as other stakeholder partners, came to understand the value of investing in a central facility that served a variety of community needs, particularly a facility with measurable, documented impact. The champion's role was to advocate for users and consistently communicate their needs.

CUSTOMIZING SERVICES—LIBRARY AS TEST BED FOR TEACHING AND RESEARCH TECHNOLOGIES

Evolving and horizon technologies can, in themselves, present opportunities. For example, in 1996, wireless technologies had not crossed many planners' radar screens. In 1999, such technologies were beginning to be considered cautiously at many libraries. Today, in 2006, wireless network access is hardly novel, and in fact is an expectation for many users as a "typical" library service.

A guiding principle behind Hardin Library's Commons was to accept a degree of reasonable risk in the ongoing experimentation with new technologies. Using wireless networking as an example, in 1999 the Commons provided an opportunity for the library and one other partner to invest in the technology at a small, controlled scale. The library was interested in extending a new service to its users, while the stakeholder partner was interested in the potential for the technology to enhance learning outcomes.

Another example of this established practice of using the Commons as a test bed (again in a partnership model) was the development of "dual-platform" access in one of the electronic classrooms. During the early, formative years of the

Commons, stakeholders considered it crucial for both Macintosh and Windows to be available for teaching. A Macintosh solution at the time provided for an add-in DOS compatibility board—and IT staff figured out how to deliver Windows 95, Windows 3.1, and the MacOS in one box.

Fast forward from 1996 to 2002: instructors who used Linux in their biomedical research activities commented on how they enjoyed teaching in the Commons, but expressed disappointment that they were only able to use Windows-based applications. The library had an interest in supporting this emerging need, but lacked the resources to move forward (other than physical facilities and hardware). In addition to the library, two additional stakeholders emerged: a faculty member who headed a biomedical computing research lab and a clinical research department with deep expertise in the development of brain-imaging applications running under Linux. These stakeholders lacked the physical facilities and computers, but possessed funding and technical expertise.

Again, collaboration sometimes requires brokering by a champion, and sometimes simply requires letting go of some control. In this example, the library agreed to give over the configuration and updating of the "Linux side" of a classroom's computers to its partners. By joining together, the library and the two stakeholder groups were able to coordinate physical facilities, hardware resources, financial supplements, and diverse IT expertise. The result: a classroom full of workstations in which a user could, at startup, opt to run either Windows or Linux as an operating system, along with specialized applications. This establishment of "choice of operating system" ultimately provided a flexible teaching environment that was beneficial to instructors who required specialized research tools.

More recent discussions about how to extend the utility of Commons spaces focused on research computing. With properly configured systems, a classroom full of computers running Linux could potentially be utilized as a test bed for grid computing. In 2006, one of the previous partner departments expressed an interest in utilizing the potential "after-hours" processing of Commons computers to focus on crunching through vast amounts of brain imagery data. Grid computing typically involves joining a number of computers to grind away at a large amount of data. By using networked desktop computers in a grid, the combined computational power offers enormous efficiencies typically found in a dedicated data-processing computer, like a supercomputer. Without a champion pouring energy into establishing the collaborative framework, most initiatives fail. Time will tell if Hardin Library will appoint a champion to pursue this collaborative effort, which would be a unique utilization of an information commons' resources for a targeted user base.

CUSTOMIZING SERVICES—
LIBRARY AS CREATOR, PRODUCER, OR PUBLISHER

By communicating frequently with users and observing trends in user activities, a library may see opportunity to develop new-breed services. A tangible example that can comfortably live within the operational framework of an advanced-technology information commons is a creation and publishing service.

At Hardin Library, such a spin-off service was founded in 1998. Information Commons Production Services (ICPS) offered collaborative, client-centered services to support the creation and delivery of educational content and information resources. By partnering with individuals and departments, ICPS extended the traditional service role of the library into more entrepreneurial ventures involving multimedia authoring, digitization, publishing, information design, and application development. ICPS empowered client self-sufficiency by offering follow-up training to enable clients to maintain technology products and/or projects themselves.

Since its founding, the Information Commons' award-winning production services unit has successfully carved out a new role for Hardin Library and the University of Iowa Libraries, and showcases the possibilities of collaboration and a spirit of entrepreneurship. By shaping a technologically flexible service and customizing its partnerships with campus clients, ICPS staff members extended the role of the library deep into learning spaces management, project management, and electronic publishing territories.

The production service did not magically appear. Again, as with any advancement of a facility's service offerings, a champion is required to cast the direction and energize the effort. Assessment of the user population, listening, and identification of emerging needs expressed by patrons requires that *someone take responsibility* for leading the charge. Within the academic health sciences environment surrounding Hardin Library, the champion recognized the emerging demand for this type of production service, determined that no other campus service was positioned to respond (answering the question: is there competition?), and refocused the activities of selected staff members as an experimental foray into the world of production and publishing.

PRODUCTION SERVICES: SCOPE OF SERVICES

Production services can be an outgrowth of a strategic effort to customize information commons services for its specific user community. At Hardin Library, these services were directed to the academic audience. Faculty members and their departments frequently create content for teaching and research purposes. In many cases, however, these individuals lacked the expertise to design databases, create multimedia assets, develop web content delivery systems, and produce other forms of digital media projects.

While the Commons served as a consultation venue and provided support for faculty or staff members who wanted to do it themselves, many individuals (with increasing demands on their time to conduct research and teach) preferred to have somebody do the digital production work for them. The typical relationship between ICPS and a "client" was a partnership—the faculty or staff member focused on the content, while the service librarians and digital media specialists focused on information design, system architecture, usability, workflow, and delivery technologies.

Information Commons Production Services unit at Hardin Library was not always a revenue-generating operation. In its early days, projects were pursued on a *pro bono* basis. However, from fiscal year 1999–2000 to late 2006, the service earned more than $80,000 through direct-bill projects, and brought in much more funding through indirect means (securing small grants, serving as a subcontractor on external grant projects, etc.). Project clients were charged not with the intention of fully recovering library costs, but instead as a means of raising the perceived value of the library's services.

When an individual or department is asked to pay for a service, psychologically the stakes go up and the investment seems more tangible and real. Paying clients tend to devote more energy to a partnership with the library and place more importance on the collaborative relationship. Communications often are more efficient when the meter is ticking. Staff members at Hardin Library learned through experience that the end product (whether it was a website redesign or database, a multimedia CD-ROM, or an electronic publication in some other form) appeared to hold more "value" to the client than if it had been created and produced without charge.

When a potential project was identified, production services staff members met with the potential client (or group) to perform an assessment. Staff members identified the core needs for the project, learned about the desired outcomes, and discussed some of the issues or barriers facing the client that may (or may not) be addressed by tackling the project. During this needs-assessment stage, the production services staff members typically provided an informal consultation. In some cases, the recommendation was, "Technology is not the answer here, no matter how much money you throw at the project."

A rate sheet to guide staff members in estimating a project's costs was developed within the first two years of the service's establishment. Staff members took information gleaned through the needs-assessment interview and matched it with the appropriate technology solution, then estimated the costs associated with developing and implementing the project.

The revenue-generating model developed at Hardin Library may or may not be one that other libraries could implement. Both the culture and fiscal environment in which a library operates must dictate the appropriate funding model for this type of service. It is important to note that ICPS was not created to be a profit maker or even a full cost-recovery operation, but instead was a subsidized service.

PRODUCTION SERVICES: STAFFING

At Hardin, the core of the production service was professional, typically staffed by a full-time digital media projects manager, two half-time graduate assistants, and a grant-funded half-time graduate assistant. Overall guidance was provided by a senior-level librarian/technologist. Additional expertise from other members of the library staff was applied to selected projects, depending on the project's scope or the skill sets best matched to the project deliverables. Those other staff members "tapped" to participate in a given project might have included a library website manager with specialized database design and reference experience, or a web services librarian.

To develop a production service, a library need not invest in a full-blown dedicated staff. Starting out on a boutique-project basis can help "test the market" for a service and can help establish a track record. The Information Commons Production Service at Hardin started out in much this way. Forty hours a week of graduate assistant work (in the form of two half-time graduate assistants) and ten hours of a professional librarian/technologist's time provided the initial investment in project work. Even dedicating a quarter of a library staff member's time to a project can yield valuable experience for starting up a service.

Key to the production services model: being open to opportunity, and accepting the role of "library as producer." A production service is nontraditional library behavior, particularly when designed to be entrepreneurial. A production service does come with some measure of reasonable (but manageable) risk. Sustainability is always a concern.

PRODUCTION SERVICES: PROJECT SELECTION CRITERIA

The benefit to a library that provides production services can be varied. Increased visibility within the community is an obvious goal, but there may be others. A library's strategic direction should inform the projected goals for production services.

At Hardin Library, ICPS management staff members determined the investment of production services resources and time to be appropriate when a project matched one or more of the following characteristics:

- project aligned with Hardin Library or institutional strategic goals;
- project had the potential for visibility and demonstrated a high likelihood for impact on the campus community and/or academic colleges/departments;
- project offered integration possibilities with broader teaching and learning trends in a given academic discipline or the higher education community overall;
- project enhanced the client's teaching and learning mission and/or research mission;
- project provided ICPS staff with practical experience using new tools or innovative technologies that potentially could be leveraged in future projects or in other creative ways.

SELECTED EXAMPLES OF PRODUCTION PROJECTS

Sometimes it is difficult to envision what form production services "outputs" can take. In this section, a few projects are briefly described, with some discussion about the outcomes and opportunities these projects offered for the Information Commons and Hardin Library.

Production of Multimedia Learning Title

A "flagship project" produced in 1998, *The Bones of the Skull: A 3-D Learning Tool* originally was a multimedia CD-ROM for Mac and Windows. This two-time national award-winning product taught skull anatomy with interactive exercises. Integrated with the textbook content were QuickTime VR anatomical models that could be manipulated, rotated, and zoomed. This project was an early example of how the library could serve as a partner with a faculty member to actually create and publish educational content. The Commons later gained practical experience in the tracking and delivery of the software to end users. The library developed an online database for individuals to request the software, which also provided data about where the software was being distributed. More than 8,000 copies were distributed worldwide—a sizeable number considering the niche content and lack of any investment in marketing or advertising for the product.[2]

The faculty stakeholder needed an entity to provide project management, technology development, and guidance in preparing instructional content. The Commons was well positioned to tackle the project because of its early experimentation with key innovative technologies, and because it employed a graduate assistant with subject expertise in instructional design and computer-based instruction.

Two Projects: Website and Database Design

An academic department contracted with ICPS to design and produce its website. The department already received server and hardware support from a central IT department; however, that department was not equipped to manage a production project like this. For ICPS, the project was envisioned as a portfolio builder, proof that the library was equipped technologically to handle production. The website project also served as an entry, or "hook," into learning more about the curricular trends of the academic department, as well as a practical opportunity to develop in-house expertise with site design and usability.

Satisfaction with the work led the department to contract with ICPS for a follow-up project more directly related to teaching and learning—a practice-question website designed to be used primarily by students in health sciences disciplines. Faculty members had already created the instructional content (22,000 questions with multiple-choice answers) and explanatory text. The department needed a delivery solution. As librarians, staff members from the Commons brought a deep understanding of how to organize information, how to structure data, and how to present content in a usable way.

Creating a Publication Workflow System and Publishing to Handheld Devices

As a health sciences library, Hardin stayed attuned to PDA trends and offered resources to help guide users. In terms of production, however, ICPS took this role a step further. Working with a nationally ranked clinical department to publish its enormous manual of head and neck surgical protocols, ICPS led developments in three "editions." First, the content was published as a web CD, then as both a web CD and a resource downloadable on Palm and Pocket PC handheld devices. In its latest version, the book was made available for handheld devices as well as on the web. What distinguished the "third edition" of the technology delivery was behind the scenes: a fully customized publishing system that allowed for peer review and editorial control of the book's content before it became published live.

The department needed a delivery solution and lacked expertise (or close access to expertise) in creating a multipurpose system for content delivery. Again, by listening to client needs, deconstructing workflows, and focusing on usable information delivery, the Commons brought "librarian-like" expertise to the project.

Resource "Discovery" Website Tailored to Public Health Professionals

The grant-funded Iowa Public Health Information website served as a national model for creating new kinds of information/research resources. The library created an easy-to-use, highly accessible website that emphasized hard-to-find local and state public health resources and provided links to National Library of Medicine (NLM) and Centers for Disease Control and Prevention (CDC) resources. The target user group for the site was public health professionals throughout the state.[3]

The back-end architecture was remarkable in that it offered content librarians full control over each of the site's pages or "records" without having to touch the interface. Content specialists data-mined the web for the best and most relevant content. At the time of its launch, the database contained more than 2,300 highly relevant records—annotated links to primary source public health content on the web. Although its pages were dynamically generated, the entire site was designed to be easily crawled by Google and other search engines, further enhancing access and avoiding a common problem where such resources often become part of the "hidden" or "deeper" web. Although this project was not a work-for-hire, it utilized many of the existing project management and technology development skills that had been developed over time within ICPS. The project involved collaboration from staff members throughout the library, bringing together the skills of collection specialists, reference expertise, and technology.

Software Development on a Small Scale

By working with instructors and faculty members on other projects and within the Information Commons learning spaces, staff members began to see a growing need for a lecture-narration solution that could utilize PowerPoint content, but offer more flexible features. This project was not one in which a single stakeholder requested service, but rather the bridging of an identified need and a staff member's creative solution.

Application development, which is daunting for many libraries, is possible given the right combination of staff skills. iLecture was a free program developed as an easy-to-use mechanism for instructors to narrate PowerPoint slides. Audio could be recorded and maintained in sequence with slide imagery. iLecture compressed audio to the MP3 format, then automatically created a convenient folder of web, image, and audio content. All the instructor (or assistant) needed to do was copy or upload that folder to a website and presto, a fully narrated, online lecture.[4]

SIDE EFFECT FOR AN INFORMATION COMMONS:
CAMPUS LEADER

Over time, given the varied activities of the Commons' physical facilities and services, the community in which the library operates will see the library as not just as a service provider, but as a leader. At the University of Iowa, the Commons became established as a key partner in teaching and learning on campus. A 2003 university initiative to assess the "state of e-learning" on campus was completed, along with a discrete recommendation to standardize on one single, centrally supported CMS (course management system). A campus-wide project, the selection of that system occurred in November 2004. The champion from the Commons occupied a key place at the table during these discussions of online teaching and learning and associated services. The champion's role was to represent the UI Libraries overall, as well as provide a conduit into the academic health science community. The importance of representing the library in this venue was not only to provide input into the technology planning initiative, but to plant the seeds for an ongoing opportunity: the integration of a wide-ranging library presence within the context of the new online course environment.

SUMMARY: REQUIREMENTS FOR CUSTOMIZING A COMMONS

Whether the initiative involves experimentation with new technology for teaching or the repurposing of space for nontraditional research activity, the commons offers an environment and opportunity for a library to invite its community of users to participate as stakeholders and co-owners. Customizing the function or service offerings of a physical facility sometimes requires giving up "control" to that community of users or to selected stakeholders who have an interest in repurposing the space. To many librarians and IT support staff members, such risk taking does not come naturally.

There are three core principles (or requirements) for customizing physical spaces or creating new services. These can be described as transferable "lessons," applicable to any library seeking to enhance its commons offerings:

1. To ease the underlying discomfort associated with the practice of "loosening control," a new collaborative effort ultimately should be guided by the relevance of the initiative to the strategic goals of the library. This applies to redesign of information commons spaces for the benefit of users, or to the repurposing of existing space for new service activities. Investment in a new initiative simply for the "cool technology" factor is wasted time if it does not bring relevance to the library's community of users.
2. Assessment of user needs and communication with stakeholders is crucial. For example, what Hardin Library offered for customization of its Information Commons facilities may not apply to other libraries' spaces. In short, a library that simply copies another library's "customization idea" without considering the individuality of its local user population, conducting a needs

assessment, and communicating with its partners may not see success in the outcomes of that initiative.

3. An identifiable champion is important to moving a customization initiative from planning to implementation. All it takes is one library staff member who has an understanding of the delicate balance between library as "authority" and library as "collaborative entity." While one person frequently is the driver behind the customization of a commons, success depends on the contributions of many staff members. A successful champion or evangelist for the development of a commons may be found at any level in the organization—a director, a manager, a service librarian, or a technology specialist. Success, however, is dependent on whether or not the umbrella library supports the fundamental mission of the commons.

Ultimately, the information commons provides a core model, but the customizations that an individual library introduces to the model are subject to the evolving needs of its user population. The best libraries understand and actively track their users. A customized information commons establishes a strong foothold for the future of libraries, addressing tangibly the question of "relevance" in the digital age, while ensuring that next generation users can depend on the foundational strengths of a library: access, information literacy, and lifelong learning.

NOTES

1. The Information Arcade was the first facility of its kind in the country, created in 1992, and was the recipient of the 1994 ALA/Meckler Library of the Future Award. The Arcade was first headed by Anita Lowry, a librarian who came to the University of Iowa from Columbia University, where she had served as deputy head of Butler Library's Reference Department and cofounder and director of the library's Electronic Text Service. She made invaluable contributions to the library profession throughout her career and was instrumental in casting an initial vision of what many institutions now are beginning to call learning commons or knowledge commons. Her vision was a place where traditional library reference services and instructional services could be successfully blended with "newer" technology-oriented consultation services and electronic resources of every format imaginable. Organizationally, the University of Iowa was moving along that path until Anita died unexpectedly during heart surgery in July 1996.

2. www.lib.uiowa.edu/commons/skullvr/

3. www.iowapublichealth.org/

4. www.lib.uiowa.edu/commons/ilecture/

II

The Field Guide

Field Guide

INTRODUCTION TO THE FIELD GUIDE ENTRIES

The field guide entries focus on those libraries that call their integrated service program or facility an "Information Commons," or one of several related terms such as "Technology Commons," "Knowledge Commons," or "Learning Commons." The key distinguishing criterion was if the service program or facility described encompassed the three spheres of: 1) new information resources; 2) collaborative service programs; and 3) reconceptualized staff and user spaces.

Each field guide entry consists of two parts, a quantitative section for summary data and a qualitative section for narrative response descriptions. To solicit this information and aid in its compilation, in 2005, the editors developed and distributed a survey (appendix A) to a select group of over a hundred academic and research libraries. The list was assembled from a literature search, a web search, suggestions from colleagues, and the editors' or authors' personal knowledge, and did not attempt to be comprehensive, or represent a systematic sample of libraries. The aim was rather to present information for a geographically distributed set of libraries that would provide a historical snapshot of current practice, and a resource for those wanting to visit one or more sites where an information commons was in place and operating.

The aim was for each entry to include at least one photograph and one floor plan, with other appropriate images as available. Respondents were given guidance on how to answer individual questions, including the typical expected range and nature of the information sought, as well as any framing information particular to the question. In the case of some quantitative questions, if respondents lacked the specific information requested, they were invited to make an informed estimate and indicate that it was an estimate.

If a project was still only in the planning stages and had not yet been implemented, it was not included. The editors made a good faith effort to follow up with those invited to respond. Data gathering, compilation, and clarification was substantially completed by the summer of 2006.

◆

BRIGHAM YOUNG UNIVERSITY
HAROLD B. LEE LIBRARY
PROVO, UTAH, USA

Total student enrollment: 30,000
Carnegie classification: Doctoral research institution
Date established: 2004
Name: Information Commons/General Reference
Square footage of the information commons area: 12,000 square feet
Total square footage of the building: 665,000 square feet
Location: Main library on the third (main) floor
Typical access hours per week: 101
Typical service hours per week: 101
Number of service points: 3
Number of computers available for use: 104
Average monthly door count: Not available
Average monthly service transactions: 7,500
Workstation sessions/logins: 50,770
Relevant URLs:
Library website: www.lib.byu.edu/
Library general software: www.lib.byu.edu/departs/gen/ic/cls.html
Multimedia software: www.lib.byu.edu/departs/gen/ic/multimedia.html

Purpose

There was a growing need for a space where groups could gather to work on academic projects without being "shhhed" by a librarian. In addition, users needed spaces with and without computers for group projects, including access to scanners and high-tech study rooms. Wired and wireless access for laptops was also desired and included in the product.

Services

The computers in the information commons are divided into four groups: individual workstations, group collaboration stations, group study rooms, and multimedia stations. Information commons staff provide assistance with multimedia issues, computer problems (including individuals' laptops), and reference/research assistance. Reference and research help were preexisting services. New

services include the multimedia and computer help, as well as the various types of computers. The general reference department was rearranged and expanded to accommodate the area's new purposes. The majority of the computers use the Microsoft Windows platform, with two multimedia computers that are Apple Macintosh. The computers support the following types of stations: individual, group collaboration, group study rooms, study tables, open, public ten-minute lookup, and multimedia.

Software

Each of the computers is reimaged every night and includes many of the most used software programs. For a detailed list of software on the general use and multimedia computers, please follow the URLs listed above. Printing is available through a Pharos system and payment is processed at a print station where money is taken from students' accounts using their student ID cards. Current charges are seven cents per page for black-and-white and twenty cents per page for color. In addition, there are two digital voice recorders, one digital still camera, and two digital video cameras available for checkout. All hardware and software are maintained by the department of Library Information Systems.

Print Resources

The majority of our print reference collection has been moved to other parts of the library due to infrequent use. The most used reference materials, such as dissertation abstracts, publisher information, encyclopedias, fact books, and software manuals, remain shelved in the Information Commons.

Staff

A corps of student workers supports computer and multimedia inquiries. Support is available from 7 a.m. to midnight, Monday through Friday, and 8 a.m. to midnight on Saturday. The facility is closed on Sunday. In addition, a full-time librarian or staff member works at the reference desk from 8 a.m. to 10 p.m., Monday through Thursday, and until 5 p.m. on Friday. The Information Commons is open and staffed whenever the library is open. The computer/multimedia assistants sup-

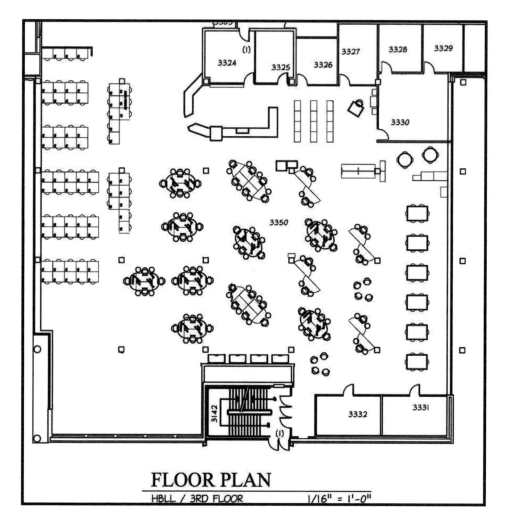

FLOOR PLAN

| HBLL / 3RD FLOOR | 1/16" = 1'-0" |

port the periodicals room during busy periods, and those employees are used as "rovers" to answer support calls that come from other parts of the library.

There is a weekly training meeting in which students are trained in customer service and the software and hardware that we support. Students are hired through the campus hiring process in the student employment office. They come from varying backgrounds, but some basic skills, such as an ability to learn new things quickly, are required in order to be hired.

Funding/Budget

The funds for the Information Commons come out of the library budget. The planning for the implementation of the Commons was a library-wide initiative. Planning and management are now performed by the Information Commons section head, under the direction of the General Information Services department chair, who reports to the associate university librarian for public services. There is enough autonomy to adapt according to the needs of the patrons who come into the area.

Publicity/Promotion

When the Information Commons opened, a lot of advertising was done to encourage people to check it out. Since then, there has not been a lot of time or effort spent on marketing. The location of the Information Commons and its reception by the students has made it a very popular space in the library. Word-of-mouth has been the best form of advertising. A marketing program is in development, especially for new items in the Commons, which will make use of the library newsletter and a campus newspaper.

Evaluation

Most feedback is by word-of-mouth from those who use the facility. There is currently no means for formally evaluating the Information Commons, but a review process is under development, to be conducted at least annually.

◄━━━

BUCKNELL UNIVERSITY
ELLEN CLARKE BERTRAND LIBRARY,
INFORMATION SERVICES AND RESOURCES (ISR)
LEWISBURG, PENNSYLVANIA, USA

Total student enrollment: 3,650
Undergraduate: 3,500
Graduate: 150
Carnegie classification: Baccalaureate college
Date established: 1999
Name: Information Services and Resources (ISR)
Square footage of the information commons area: Unable to provide a precise estimate of the Information Commons area because it is more conceptual in nature and spans across the public service areas of the library
Square footage of the building: 103,000 square feet
Location: Main level of Bertrand Library
Typical access hours per week: 100+
Typical service hours per week: 100+
Number of service points: 3
Number of computers available for use: 64
Average monthly door count: Total gate count for library, 248,343 (Fall 2004); 230,257 (Spring 2005)
Average monthly service transactions: The average number of transactions at the technology support desk is 3,149 per year.
Workstation sessions/logins: Not available

Relevant URLs:
Bertrand Library floor plan: www.bucknell.edu/x11287.xml

Purpose

ISR's Information Commons was conceptualized and designed during the two years following the administrative merger of Bucknell University's library, technology, and media services. ISR also desired to create a service environment that better represented its merged technology and library services, with the understanding that users did not work or produce in isolation of the array of support services that ISR could provide for them. ISR's goal was to provide more seamless "one-stop shopping" for users' technology and information needs, while increasing access to public services that had previously been obscured either by location or limited service hours.

ISR conducted an inventory of services in order to identify technology and library services that should remain intact, and services that should be merged or reconfigured to create the Information Commons (IC). Services were categorized and ranked according to their public service nature and whether they needed to be moved to a more prominent location for users. It made sense to disband or merge some services, while making others more publicly accessible to users. Creating ISR's IC was as much a new service concept as it was a renovation of physical space in the library building to accommodate the final design.

"Information Commons" was the name used by Information Services and Resources in 1999 to describe its renovation and introduction of a new service point on the main level of the library building to support technology and media services. "Information Commons" is rarely used by either the campus or ISR staff to describe its service vision. Most often, tour guides and staff describe the IC concept by naming the individual service points of circulation/reserves/equipment, reference/information desk, and technology support desk. The ISR web pages indicate that the Information Commons is the technology support desk and its adjoining technology courtyard.

Services

The Information Commons service was designed within the existing public service space on the main level of the Bertrand Library building. The computing "help desk" and the media services department were disbanded and merged to form a new service point called the technology support desk. (Originally, this service desk was called the "technology/media services desk" and its purpose was not only computing support, but also equipment loans. Approximately two years ago, media services support was removed and transferred to the circulation/reserves desk/equipment desk.) A technology courtyard with collaborative work spaces and specialized equipment, software, and a film editing suite was built in the area adjoining the technology support desk.

The existing traditional library service points for reference, circulation, and reserves were reviewed during the IC's planning stages. The reference services area was reconfigured to accommodate more computers that would be "open" not only for researching, but to the university's licensed software. The reference/information desk was also redesigned to provide staff and users with a consultation area for extended reference. The IC's design represented ISR's commitment to providing quality services in a physical environment that gave users convenient access to technology and information support.

Software

Machines in the technology courtyard adjoining the technology support desk are imaged with Microsoft Office products, Dreamweaver, Flash, Fireworks, C++, desktop publishing software, and several software products related to course support. Both Macs and PCs are available in the courtyard and scanners are available at each machine. Machines in the research services area are imaged with Microsoft Office products and allow access to most university-licensed software products; eight to ten machines are reserved for guest login.

Software support is offered through the technology support desk, the reference/information desk (according to staff abilities to troubleshoot), or by appointment with either ISR staff or technology student assistants.

Print Resources

The Information Commons service points and equipment and the library's print reference collection coexist on the main level of the Bertrand Library. Print periodicals and microforms are located one floor above the main level. No formal evaluation of the impact of technology services on the use of printed resources has been done at ISR. General knowledge and observation of users' work habits indicate a steady increase in demand for electronically available materials, particularly journals, even if the user is working in the library building. Library staff believe that this increase is due to users' expectations for quick, convenient retrieval of materials to support their research rather than any of the services that the Information Commons is able to provide to them.

Staff

Each service point hires and trains its own staff. There are very few instances of staff cross training among service desks, but this may not be the case as ISR continues to evolve as an integrated information and technology services organization. An Information Commons assistant position was once shared between the reference/information and technology support desks. As reference activity decreased and technology support needs increased, this position grew entirely into a technology support position. The result is that technology support desk staff need to staff the technology service point consistently to keep current and competent at troubleshooting users' technology needs.

The reference/information desk has a history of providing opportunities for nonlibrarian staff to be trained to assist users at the service desk. The technology support desk took a similar approach to staffing its service point, but the nature of the work required a full commitment to technology support work. All three service desks rely on student assistants to provide much of the front-end staff-

ing. Undergraduate student assistants are hired for the technology support and circulation/reserves/equipment desks, while the reference/information desk employs only graduate student assistants. All service points train students to refer appropriate questions among the service desks.

Roving does not occur in the Information Commons or general public service area. Users are encouraged to schedule tutoring or one-on-one appointments with librarians or other ISR staff to assist them with their work. It is ISR's policy to provide staffing at all service desks whenever the library building is open.

Funding/Budget

There is no separate budget line for the Information Commons.

Publicity/Promotion

Prior to physical renovation for the IC, ISR met with students, staff, and faculty groups for their input about the concept of the Information Commons. A campus open house was held at the completion of the project to introduce the new services.

Evaluation

There has been no comprehensive assessment of the ISR or Information Commons. The LibQUAL+ survey has provided valuable information regarding the quality of services and availability of equipment provided by all public service desks. ISR has also used focus groups, user interviews, and other assessment measures to track how well it meets users' information and technology needs.

◆

CALIFORNIA STATE POLYTECHNIC UNIVERSITY (CAL POLY)
ROBERT E. KENNEDY LIBRARY
SAN LUIS OBISPO, CALIFORNIA, USA

Total student enrollment: 2005–2006: 18,000
Undergraduate: 17,000
Graduate: 1,000
Carnegie classification: Master's college or university
Date established: Fall 2005
Name: The Learning Commons or the Digital Teaching Library (DTL)
Square footage of the information commons area: Phase I is 5,445 square feet; Phase II is in the planning stages and may be an additional 35,000 square feet.
Square footage of the building: 200,000 square feet
Location: Main library; northwest section of second floor
Typical access hours per week: 100
Typical service hours per week: 100
Number of service points: 2

Number of computers available for use: 77 in the Learning Commons. Other comput-
ing or computer-assisted research consultation facilities in the library offer an
additional 100 computers.
Average monthly door count: Not available
Average monthly service transactions: Not available
Workstation sessions/logins: Not available
Relevant URLs:
Learning Commons website: http://learningcommons.lib.calpoly.edu/

Purpose

The Learning Commons, built by Instructional Technology Services (ITS) and
the Robert E. Kennedy Library, provides all library users with access to a modern
collaborative work space that is complete with the latest technological, print, nonprint, and human resources tailored to active learning communities. As part of
the Digital Teaching Library (DTL) initiative, this flexible, multiuse space accommodates teaching with technology, promotes cross-disciplinary social interactions
that encourage academic and intellectual pursuits, promotes collaborative projects, and creates a sense of community where students and faculty both contribute
to and benefit from a knowledge creation and dissemination process.

The DTL initiative provides Cal Poly with a new physical and virtual facility
that offers faculty and students a powerful new teaching and learning resource
with the capacity to foster creative and flexible interactions and learning relationships among students, faculty, resources, and technology.

Services

The Learning Commons is a multiyear project. In the initial stage, ITS computer labs were transferred to the second floor of the Kennedy Library in close proximity to knowledge managers, a service desk/learning hub, and the adaptive technology center. PC and Macintosh labs were moved during spring and summer 2005. A high-end faculty research facility that currently hosts a virtual reality research and instructional project will also introduce new computer-aided interdisciplinary instruction. An integrated mobile computing service allows students to check out and use laptops, thus encouraging flexible, informal collaboration.

These classrooms/labs will provide the technological infrastructure for the collaborative learning communities to be developed in phase two. The reference desk and reference room, equipped with nearly forty computers, is reconfigured to allow for more in-depth and individualized research assistance from library staff.

Software

Central IT services provides support and infrastructure of software, including imaging of workstations, Adaptec CD Creator 5.0, Adobe, Acrobat Distiller 6.0, Acrobat Professional 6.0, Acrobat Reader 6.0, Illustrator CS, ImageReady CS, In-Design CS, PageMaker 7.0, Photoshop CS, Premier 6.5, Aquifer 2.0, Autodesk, 3ds max 5 (discreet), Architectural Desktop 2004, AutoCAD 2004, Map 5, Mechanical Desktop 2004, VIZ 4, Cadence PSD 15.0, Capture CIS, IntelliCAD 2001, Layout Plus, PSpice AD, PSpice Advanced Analysis, PSpice Optimizer, Schematics, Diet Analysis Plus 6.1, EAI FactoryView, EDS FactoryCAD, ESRI, ArcGIS 9, ArcInfo Workstation, ArcView GIS 9, Spatial Analyst 2.0, Fathom 1.16, Form Z 4.0.0, Garden Graphics, DynaScape, QuoteScapes, Haestad Methods, CulvertMaster, Graphical HEC-1, HEC-HMS, HEC-RAS, SewerCAD, StormCAD, WaterCAD, JCreator LE 2.5, Macromedia, Contribute 2.0, Director MX, Dreamweaver MX 2004, Fireworks MX 2004, Flash MX 2004, FreeHand 10, MatLab 7, Microsoft (Access, Excel, Internet Explorer 6, PowerPoint, Visual Studio .NET, Word), Minitab 14, Mozilla 1.5, Netscape 7.1, ProModel 4.23, Putty, QvtTerm 5.1, S-PLUS 6.2 release, SAS 2.6 for ver. 8, SPSS 12.0, VectorWorks, Visual ModFlow 2.8.2, and WS_FTP LE 5.08.

Print Resources

The DTL Learning Commons is currently adjacent to the library stacks. In phase two, the stacks will be pushed back. New, low-lying bookshelves will be integrated with print reference materials that target all schools and fields taught at the university, intermingled with computing resources and informal seating.

Staff

Based on the University of Southern California's student navigation assistants model, Learning Commons consultants (LCCs) will be hired by the library and central IT Services (ITS). LCCs will be trained in technology and information, as well as communications competence, and will provide both navigational assistance and

CAL POLY

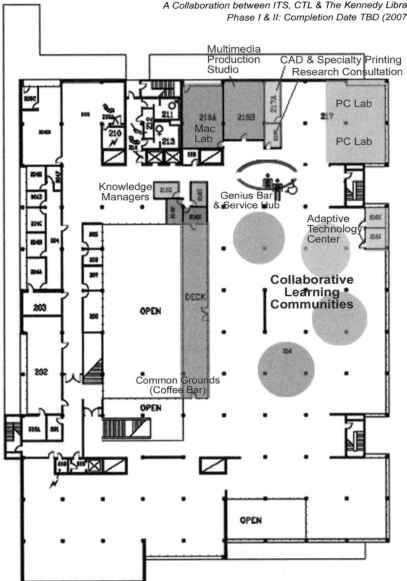

Multimedia Production Studio

CAD & Specialty Printing
Research Consultation

PC Lab

PC Lab

Mac Lab

Knowledge Managers

Genius Bar & Service Hub

Adaptive Technology Center

Collaborative Learning Communities

OPEN

DECK

203

202

OPEN

Common Grounds (Coffee Bar)

OPEN

OPEN

technical support. Limited application support may be provided by LCCs, although all student and permanent employees will be encouraged to seek appropriate application training. LCCs are being recruited from student computing committees, computer science, and new media courses.

LCCs are responsible for the security and monitoring of the lab facility during all main library hours. LCCs will be trained in-house by the library and ITS staff, who have constructed a detailed training program. ITS and the library seek to create and implement a highly competitive student internship program that will include recruitment of student interns dedicated to the Commons during the three-year pilot project. Students will be trained in information and communications competency, information technology, and printing services through a combination of training provided by Cal Poly's full-time staff and on-the-job training in support of Cal Poly's "learn by doing" model. Learning Commons consultants will be required to commit to a year-long credit-bearing paid internship. Highly skilled and motivated students will undergo thorough and rigorous training and successful completion of milestones.

Funding/Budget

Construction for the Learning Commons is generously sponsored by the Cal Poly Minor Capital Outlay Program. The library and ITS have partnered to fund additional start-up costs as well as ongoing operations and staffing.

Publicity/Promotion

Library faculty will work closely with faculty who teach in the Learning Commons, as well as other highly motivated "early adopters" of technology on campus, to integrate information competence into the curriculum and to help faculty take full advantage of the resources available in both the DTL Learning Commons and the library as a whole. General public awareness strategies include, but are not limited to, a website, library tours, student orientation, referrals from other service points in the library, and word-of-mouth/viral marketing.

Evaluation

User statistics will be measured. Additional feedback will be provided by the annual library survey and annual reviews of computing facilities and resources conducted by a myriad of campus computing committees.

◆

EMORY UNIVERSITY
ROBERT W. WOODRUFF LIBRARY
ATLANTA, GEORGIA, USA

Total student enrollment: 11,000
Carnegie classification: Doctoral research institution

Date established: 1998
Name: Information Commons (formal), InfoCommons (colloquial)
Square footage of the information commons area: 15,000 square feet
Total square footage of the building: 300,000 square feet
Location: Main library; entrance floor and other floors
Typical access hours per week: 140
Typical service hours per week: 80
Number of service points: 3
Number of computers available for use: 240
Average monthly door count: 110,000
Average monthly service transactions: 2,400 user interactions
Workstation sessions/logins: 54,573 monthly logins
Relevant URLs:
Infocommons website: http://infocommons.emory.edu/

Purpose

The Information Commons (InfoCommons hereafter) was designed as a comprehensive new public computing service program for the Center for Library and Information Resources (CLAIR), a 1998 expansion and renovation of the Robert W. Woodruff Library, Emory University's main library complex. The InfoCommons featured a much larger number of public workstations than the library had ever previously deployed, spread throughout all levels of the Woodruff Library, with support personnel integrated into and coordinated with traditional service points.

The InfoCommons was designed to provide a new level of computing functionality for library users, enabling not only simple gathering of citations from online catalogs, but a comprehensive suite of software for sophisticated information processing. The InfoCommons concept was developed by a committee of librarians and technology specialists who studied the information technology needs of students in a range of learning activities. Providing students with greatly improved access to computing tools for library research through the InfoCommons service program was seen as critical to the success of the CLAIR.

Services

A new service point was created in 1998 for technical assistance with InfoCommons workstations. This service point operates in conjunction with (and is physically part of) the main reference desk. After 1999, two additional service points were created on different levels of the Woodruff Library to provide assistance at peak hours of facility use. These service points are located in proximity to other traditional library service points, such as the main circulation desk. InfoCommons support staff is composed primarily of students, who are trained jointly by the library's reference department and desktop systems support team. InfoCommons students are managed in their front-line support activities by a member of the reference department, who closely coordinates their operations with the regular public reference service program.

Software

From the program's inception in 1998, all InfoCommons workstations were configured with a comprehensive set of software tools. This tool set has always included, at minimum, a web browser, the campus e-mail client, a variety of specialized library applications, and the entire Microsoft Office suite. Over time, the tools included on InfoCommons workstations have been expanded to include various web plug-ins, statistics packages, and other specialized software. All software is supported by InfoCommons student assistants. Networked laser printers are located strategically throughout the facility for the convenience of InfoCommons users. Users are charged ten cents per printed page, with fees charged against their campus debit cards.

Print Resources

The InfoCommons is a distributed facility, with workstations located throughout the Woodruff Library and interspersed with the main primary collections of reference, government documents, and microforms. The philosophy that guides this integration is that the close proximity of information technology enhances patron access and use of such materials.

Staff

InfoCommons students are present at the main reference desk at all times that reference librarians staff the desk, day and night, and on weekends. Students are primarily undergraduates, and are selected for both their technical aptitude and public service attitude. Students receive a one-week training orientation to support duties in the InfoCommons, as well as periodic refresher sessions.

The reference librarians and paraprofessionals who serve as InfoCommons coordinators have varied backgrounds. They manage students, revise policies, coordinate with both the reference department and desktop support team, and provide second-tier troubleshooting for user problems that students are unable to resolve.

The desktop support staff who maintain and cultivate the InfoCommons technical infrastructure are senior IT professionals with strong backgrounds in client/server systems. They test, configure, and support the workstations and servers that comprise the infrastructure of the InfoCommons. This staff serves as third-tier support for technical problems that the InfoCommons coordinator is unable to resolve.

Funding/Budget

The budget for the InfoCommons is divided into two annually recurring parts: 1) $150,000 in funding provided by the library for staff; and 2) $150,000 in funding provided by the campus IT division for replacement computers and purchase of other needed technical infrastructure components. These amounts have been stable since 1998.

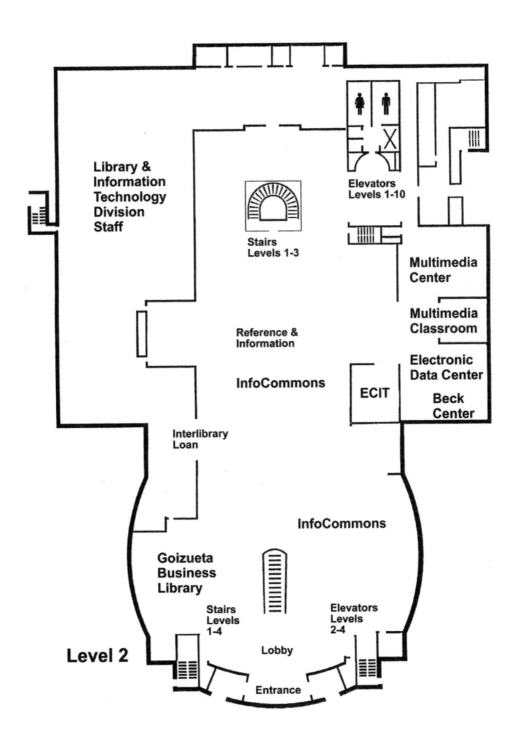

Library & Information Technology Division Staff

Stairs Levels 1-3

Elevators Levels 1-10

Reference & Information

InfoCommons

Multimedia Center

Multimedia Classroom

Electronic Data Center

ECIT

Beck Center

Interlibrary Loan

InfoCommons

Goizueta Business Library

Stairs Levels 1-4

Elevators Levels 2-4

Level 2

Lobby

Entrance

Publicity/Promotion

The InfoCommons is featured on library freshman orientation tours, and training sessions are conducted at the start of each academic year. There is no formal publicity program focused on the InfoCommons; students are primarily aware of the facility and its service offerings through word-of-mouth advertising.

Evaluation

No formal evaluation program is conducted for the InfoCommons. The main measures of success are the usage statistics, which demonstrate extremely heavy usage of the facility, especially during midterms and finals. Satisfaction is gauged informally through verbal feedback from users and other anecdotal evidence.

FERRIS STATE UNIVERSITY
FERRIS LIBRARY FOR INFORMATION, TECHNOLOGY, AND EDUCATION (FLITE)
BIG RAPIDS, MICHIGAN, USA

Total student enrollment: 11,803
Carnegie classification: Master's college or university
Date established: 2001
Name: Information Commons
Square footage of the information commons area: 9,660 square feet
Square footage of the building: 173,484 square feet
Location: Main library; entrance and second level
Typical access hours per week: 97
Typical service hours per week: 97
Number of service points: 4
Number of computers available for use: Approximately 140
Average monthly door count: 37,463 (fiscal year 2005)
Average monthly service transactions: 335
Workstation sessions/logins: Not available
Relevant URLs:
Library website: www.ferris.edu/library/

Purpose

The Information Commons (IC) at Ferris State University became a reality and an instant hit with students in March 2001 when the university opened a brand-new five-level library and digital information center that nearly tripled the size of the vacated facility. The Ferris State University Library for Information, Technology and Education, or FLITE for short, serves as the communication, cultural, and social hub on campus. As a focal point, the spacious, comfortable, and highly visible Information Commons consists of two parts—nearly 100 networked computers on the main level, and another 20 in each of two areas on the second level, which can be thought of as the "upper commons." The IC inspires users to expand

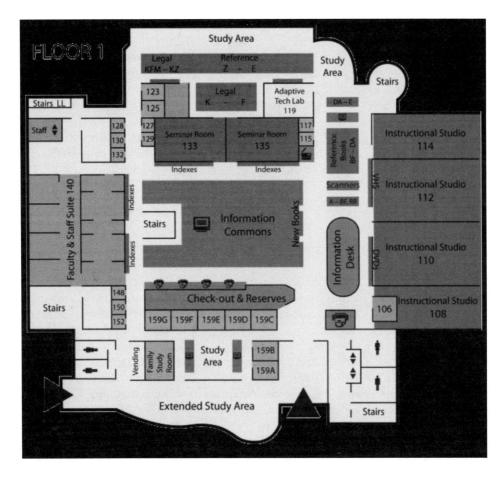

their knowledge and expertise in information access, to collaborate with peers, and to use the resulting understandings to produce new information products. Connectivity is available for users to plug in their own laptops in this environment, which includes wireless as an option.

Ferris State University is nationally known for combining theory with hands-on experiences to make its graduates immediately employable and capable of professional growth. The Information Commons was designed as an informal learning space to support this tradition with the best possible access to technologically rich local and global information resources.

Services

For sustainability, four distinct service points are within users' easy reach. During the primary semesters, the reference desk is staffed with two librarians Monday through Thursday, and on a single basis Friday through Sunday, a long-standing practice. The reference librarians partner with classroom faculty on innovative teaching and learning, as well as supporting their scholarship and service. An information desk near the entrance was established for library assistants to

answer initial inquiries and to refer users to reference librarians for in-depth research or computer support personnel, as needed. Technical computer assistance
is provided at a desk contiguous to the larger commons. Support staff in this area
are primarily students who work at all times the IC is open. The Technical Assistance Center (TAC), which is the centralized computer support desk for all Ferris
faculty and staff across campus, is in a room adjacent to the support staff work
area. Part of its function is to oversee these student assistants. Since the "upper
commons" is housed on the periodicals floor, the periodicals information desk
library assistant serves in this capacity for referral services. In the library faculty's
and staff's view, the activities at these points are the first priority.

Software

   All of the Information Commons workstations, with the exception of five computers, are configured for full service, and have an identical basic software load
that consists of Microsoft Office suite, e-mail access, web browsers, and library
proprietary databases (some databases are in-house use only). For each of the
university's colleges, there is a unique feature that allows faculty to select specialized software to support their curricula for mounting on a subset of workstations
grouped together. Although the five computers provide access to Microsoft Office
and Internet Explorer, these machines also include Adobe products for students
enrolled in the visual design and web media program. Outside of TAC's office
area are workstations with Macromedia, scanning, burning, and audio and video
editing capabilities. Across the way, the Adaptive Technologies Lab is filled with
computers and software designed for patrons who require disability services.
Networked laser printers are accessible with a copy card, and since many subscription databases enable the user to send articles to his or her personal e-mail
account, printing has become virtually trouble free. This is a remarkable improvement from the past. An outside vendor maintains this service.

Print Resources

   FLITE's ever-expanding innovative technological access is blended with print
collections. Computer stations are in close proximity to the collections. Workstation usage does not require either authentication or advance registration. If all
workstations are in use, library instruction studios on the first level are opened.
Once a user has identified a needed print item, signage and other learning aids
are readily available, or a service provider can be asked for guidance in locating
materials and setting up microform reader-printers, if necessary.

Staff

   Prior to moving into FLITE, reference librarians had planned to rove, as this
was common practice in the predecessor library. What emerged from clientele
was the desire to work anonymously, and often with peers. Due to the IC's busy-
ness, users feared they would lose their workstations if they left them unattended
for even a minute.

At the same time, new technologies were introduced, including the Live Person chat service in September 2002. Though chat was initially offered to accommodate off-campus students' needs, in the first year of operation, approximately 43 to 50 percent of the requests for assistance came from within the building, presumably from the Information Commons, where almost all public-access computers are housed. Chat became a popular option, and has been expanded to all the hours reference librarians staff the desk, including weekends. It enables users to continue multitasking—which is often a Net Generation preference—while the librarian seeks the information in order to provide guidance in filling the request at hand. By no means is chat limited to reference work only. There have been times that the computer help desk personnel have been engaged to answer questions that require their expertise.

The TAC staff have educational backgrounds in computer information systems, and several staff members have appropriate technical certification. For all FLITE faculty and staff, there is emphasis on professional development in IT, as well as with library functions. Reference and instructional librarians, moreover, participate in development programs through the Faculty Center for Teaching and Learning, and similar programming is offered through professional associations, LOEX and WILU.

Funding/Budget

Like other facets of the Information Commons, administration of the area has also evolved. Currently, there are two reporting structures: the reference faculty librarians and library assistants report to the library assistant dean; the computer help desk staff's work is overseen within the university's Administration and Finance Division, where TAC reports.

The budget is derived through an allocation process from two major sources: the Academic Affairs Division, and the Administration and Finance Division. These funds are earmarked for staffing the computer support help desk, as well as the maintenance and replacement of computers, and software upgrades. For 2005 to 2006, all of the computers in the Commons were replaced for the first time since FLITE opened. Financial support for subscription databases comes through the library.

Publicity/Promotion

One of the highlights of the campus visit for prospective students and their families is a student-led tour, complete with a walk-through of FLITE's main level featuring the Information Commons. From the beginning, we have been impressed with comments made by these students who find the Commons to be "awesome" when they first see it. This initial visit is followed with a more in-depth librarian-led tour of FLITE for our new students in the required freshman seminar course, usually during the first semester of enrollment. Some students are surprised with the multiple levels, as they have never been in a library of this size. Many candidates for faculty positions learn about the IC as part of the interview process. Faculty members discover more about the potential for integrating the

IC in teaching and learning through a long-standing liaison program. For both students and faculty, descriptive information about its services is always available at the point of need. What students, faculty, staff, and visitors from around the world see and hear when they tour the facility is the primary publicity.

Evaluation

Evaluation and assessment of FLITE services is based upon multiple quantitative and qualitative measures. Users are encouraged to evaluate services by using the suggestion box located near the Information Commons, e-mail reference, student-initiated surveys, or other appropriate means. Their comments have factored into decisions for change. Through student government, for example, student leaders passed a resolution that led to the diversification of computer hardware to support specific curricula. From these measures, FLITE staff are most interested in developing an awareness of the level of student engagement in learning, and how to better integrate pedagogy, learning space, and technology as the pathway for students to succeed now and in the future.

◆

GEORGIA INSTITUTE OF TECHNOLOGY
GEORGIA TECH LIBRARY
ATLANTA, GEORGIA, USA

Total student enrollment: 16,600
Carnegie classification: Doctoral research institution
Date established: August 2002
Name: Library West Commons (LWC)
Square footage of the information commons area: 9,500 square feet
Square footage of the building: 230,000 square feet
Location: Main library; first floor west
Typical access hours per week: 135
Typical service hours per week: 135
Number of service points: 3
Number of computers available for use: 106
Average monthly door count: 74,000
Average monthly service transactions: 1,836
Workstation sessions/logins: No session statistics; 106 computers in Commons each average 3,200 hours of use per year.
Relevant URLs:
Library West Commons information page: http://librarycommons.gatech.edu/

Purpose

The Library West Commons (LWC) is viewed as the first of several experiments to inform the design and construction of an undergraduate learning center on campus. The goal of the center is to improve undergraduate education and

retention by gathering in one location the critical resources and expertise needed for undergraduate success. The LWC was created as a partnership between the library and the Office of Information Technology to offer resources, services, and high-end support to the campus community at a "one-stop" centralized service and productivity point. Users previously moved among the library, OIT labs, and dormitory study halls to do their work. The LWC offers a comprehensive service point with improved technology offerings, expert assistance, and safe work and study space, all of which enhances students' ability to work collaboratively and to develop and present technologically enhanced projects. The LWC includes: reliable hardware; an extensive suite of productivity software, multimedia tools and specialized subject applications; course-specific tutoring; and available experts in technical support, multimedia creation, and information content, sustained in a safe environment that rarely closes.

Services

The Information Services desk (reference) is located on the edge of the Commons, incorporating three separate reference points that existed before the creation of the Commons. The Information Services department expanded its service to a 24/5 environment (135 hours per week) from 98 hours per week, in recognition that students have technology and information needs around the clock. The entire library is now on a 24/5 schedule and is staffed during the late-shift hours by Information Services, Circulation, and Security departments.

The Productivity Area has eighty-four computers (seventy-four Dell PCs and ten iMac G5s). Service existed previously in several campus labs. The change is in the high level of user support offered.

In the Multimedia Center , there are twenty-two high-end PowerMac G5s and Dells. Service existed previously for faculty and was rarely used. The change is in providing the service for students, with superior user support.

Software

The LWC Productivity Area provides software to facilitate the productivity and research needs of the institute. Included are general productivity software (Microsoft Office, LaTeX), communication software (Internet Explorer, Firefox, Trillian/Fire), specialized software in engineering (AutoCAD, PSpice, SolidEdge, TecPlot), chemistry (SciFinder Scholar, Beilstein), and mathematics and statistics (Maple, Mathematica, Matlab, R, S-Plus). A number of computer programming environments are also available (MS Visual Studio .NET, Dr. Java, Dr.Scheme, jCreator, jGrasp, Eclipse, NetBeans, Apple Developer Tools).

The LWC Multimedia Center provides software for 3-D modeling, graphics design, web publishing, web authoring, and video production. Software for this specialized lab of twenty-two high-end Dell and PowerMac G5 computers includes Adobe Creative Suite (Acrobat, GoLive, Illustrator, InDesign, Photoshop), Adobe Premier, iMovie, Final CutPro Studio, gMax, Macromedia Studio (Dreamweaver, Fireworks, Flash, Freehand), Maya, and SolidEdge.

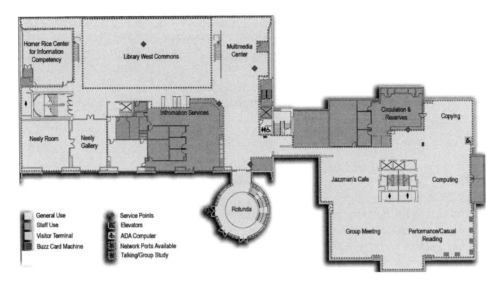

Print Resources

Print resources in the Commons include a ready reference collection (330 items) adjacent to the Information Services desk and two small collections of books that support the Productivity Area and Multimedia Center. The reference collection, microforms and maps, and current periodicals are on the second floor (one floor above the Library West Commons).

Staff

The Information Services desk (reference) is staffed all hours the library is open (135 hours per week during the academic year), primarily with Information Services department staff (eleven librarians and seven support staff). Other regular staffing is provided by an additional eleven librarians and six library career staff.

The Productivity Area is staffed from 7:30 p.m. to 4 p.m. by one full-time Office of Information Technology (OIT) staff member, who hires, trains, and supervises several student user assistants (UA) who work in the area. One UA is on duty at a time at a workstation in the middle of the area, from 8 a.m. to midnight Monday through Thursday, 8 a.m. to 6 p.m. Friday, 9 a.m. to 6 p.m. on Saturday, and noon to midnight on Sunday. The UA is expected to rove.

The Multimedia Center is staffed from 9 a.m. to 6 p.m. by one full-time OIT staff member who hires, trains, and supervises student interns in the center. The center is staffed by interns from 8 a.m. to midnight Monday through Thursday, 8 a.m. to 6 p.m. Friday, 9 a.m. to 6 p.m. on Saturday, and noon to midnight on Sunday. Multiple interns may be on duty at the same time depending on customer demand; interns are expected to rove.

Library Information Services staff offer assistance in both the Productivity Area and Multimedia Center from midnight to 8 a.m. and provide oversight for the user assistants and interns during evening hours when full-time OIT staff are not available. A new series of library positions, Information Associate I, II, and III, was created for the evening, night, and weekend shifts. The positions incorporate both library and IT skills.

Academic department teaching assistants schedule "office hours" at consultation cubicles in the LWC, for a total of approximately 150 hours per semester.

Funding/Budget

The LWC is governed by an LWC advisory council composed of two library and three OIT staff members: 1) associate director for Public Services (library); 2) head of Information Services (library); 3) program advisor (OIT) who manages the Productivity Area in the Commons; 4) a systems support specialist (OIT) who manages classroom and lab support at the Institute; and 5) the director of Information Tech Services (OIT).

The library is responsible for the physical maintenance of the LWC and provides the staffing at the Information Services desk. OIT funds two full-time LWC positions, student user assistants and interns, and positions that offer behind-the-scenes technical support for the LWC, including imaging and hardware and software maintenance. Thirty months into operation of the LWC, the library and OIT successfully applied for institute technology fee funds to refresh computing and printing hardware and peripherals.

Publicity/Promotion

There have been several articles about the LWC in the *Whistle* (faculty/staff newspaper) and *Technique* (student newspaper). In addition, new additions to the LWC, such as a presentation rehearsal studio, have been advertised in *Technique*. A variety of presentations about the LWC have been made to campus groups, both formally and informally, by the library dean, associate directors, subject librarians, and OIT staff.

Subject librarians include LWC information in their classes and orientations for students. In fall 2002, a faculty open house was held in the LWC. The LWC is highlighted in annual tours provided to incoming first-year students and their families, annual tours to prospective presidential scholars and their families, and in an annual library welcome event. Information about the LWC is included in incoming freshmen packets. The LWC is one of the campus sites for incoming first-year student registration and is the site for the Center for Excellence in Teaching and Learning's "Teaching Fellows" day, where faculty projects are highlighted. The Multimedia Center hosts the annual iMovieFest.

Evaluation

Two LWC surveys have been conducted. The results from a paper-based survey in fall 2002 (95 respondents) and an electronic survey for spring 2003 (321 respondents) were both highly positive. The comments from two LibQUAL+ Surveys conducted in 2003 and 2004 provided additional positive reinforcement about LWC services and resources. During the first year of LWC operations, several instant polls, which were limited to "yes/no" questions only, provided some assessment. Surveys and polls have been discontinued to avoid overwhelming students.

In addition, 839 questions and comments have been submitted since a "Tell Us" customer comment button was added to the library's website in September 2002. The comments pertain to the LWC, as well as other library issues. A number of changes have emerged from the "Tell Us" feature, such as the purchase of new software, corrections to malfunctioning equipment, and changes in policies.

An online tally sheet was implemented on July 1, 2003, which has resulted in more consistent statistics being taken for inquiries and activities at the Information Services desk, the Productivity Area, the Multimedia Center, and virtual reference. In 2004, students voted the LWC "the best improvement to campus" during a year in which the institute invested $250,000,000 in new and renovated buildings.

Indiana University
Herman B. Wells Library
Bloomington, Indiana, USA

Total student enrollment: 39,000
Undergraduate: 31,000
Graduate: 8,000
Carnegie classification: Doctoral research institution
Date established: The first floor opened in August 2003; the second floor opened in March 2005.
Name: Information Commons (formal), IC (colloquial)
Square footage of the information commons area: First floor is 27,000 square feet; second floor is 8,000 square feet.
Total square footage of the building: 600,000 square feet
Location: Main library; First and second floor of the west tower
Typical access hours per week: First floor, 168 hours; second floor, 117 hours
Typical service hours per week: First floor, 168 hours; second floor, 117 hours
Number of service points: 3
Number of computers available for use: 355
Average monthly door count: 150,000
Average monthly service transactions: Not available
Workstation sessions/logins: 83,000
Relevant URLs:
Information Commons website: www.libraries.iub.edu/index.php?pageId=310

Purpose

The Indiana University (IU) Information Commons (IC) was designed to enhance student learning and research by providing state-of-the-art technology and resources in an academic environment, which supports both collaborative work

and individual quiet study. The IC is a partnership between the IU Libraries and University Information Technology Services.

Services

Previously offered services—library reference and software help/consulting—are centrally located on both floors of the IU IC. Both of these services were offered in the library space prior to the IC, but not from the same service desk. The reference and software help/consulting is referred to as the reference desk. In addition, Library Instructional Services, Adaptive Technology Center, Writing Tutorial Services, and Library Circulation were all in existence in the library before the IU IC was created.

New IC services—IT account support and hardware—are now located with library circulation services at the same service counter at the entrance to the IU IC. The hardware and IT account support did not previously exist in the library. The same unit that provides this support operates a twenty-four-hour IT help line for the campus from the IU IC.

Software

The workstations in the IU IC offer over 180 software applications, including all Microsoft Office products, a wide range of multimedia software, utility applications, and statistics programs. The desktop is delivered by the Student Technology Center (STC), a unit of University Information Technology Services. The STC hardware, software, infrastructure, and human resources are supported through student technology fees.

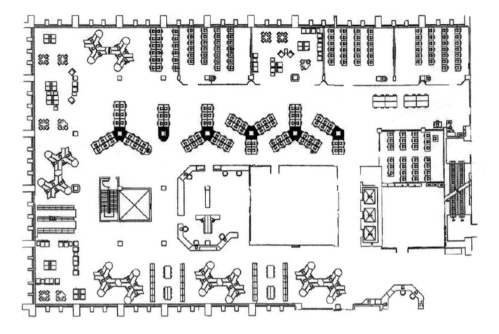

Print Resources

The IU IC1 offers the reference collection, which includes general, software, and career reference materials. The collection is housed on short shelving units near the reference desk, intermingled among workstation and study tables. The career materials and software manuals get the highest amount of use in the collection. The IU IC2 houses the undergraduate core collection of circulating, high-use materials with a short loan length of two weeks. This 17,000-volume collection is housed on a combination of short and tall shelving units.

Staff

The Information Commons Undergraduate Services (formerly the Undergraduate Library Services) department provides library reference services. The reference staff includes librarians, support staff, and graduate student hourly employees. The hours of reference services during the academic year are as follows: Sunday, 11 a.m. to midnight (librarians on duty 2 p.m. to 10 p.m.); Monday through Thursday, 8 a.m. to midnight (librarians on duty 8 a.m. to 10 p.m.); Friday, 8 a.m. to 9 p.m. (librarians on duty 8 a.m. to 5 p.m.); Saturday, 10 a.m. to 9 p.m.

The software IT consultants (Student Technology Center consultants) are undergraduate hourly student employees. They are hired, trained, and managed by full-time staff of the Student Technology Centers, and can be scheduled to work in any of the computer labs on campus or in the Information Commons. At least two consultants are on duty twenty-four hours a day.

The hardware and IT account support services are provided by the University Information Technology Services Support Center (UITS SC), which is staffed by a combination of hourly and full-time staff who are all hired, trained, and managed by UITS SC full-time staff. The service location in the Information Commons is one of two locations on campus where students, faculty, and staff can get walk-in assistance. The service hours during the academic year are typically until midnight during the week.

Library circulation services are provided by the library's Customer and Access Services Department (CASD). This is primarily staffed by an undergraduate student hourly employee who is trained by the full-time staff of the CASD department. The service hours during the academic year are typically until 2 a.m.

Funding/Budget

Each unit within the partnership funds its own staff and resources. There are no common funds. When new materials or staff are needed, the units work through their own budget lines to secure funding. In instances where common items, such as supplies, printers, public furniture, or tables are needed, the Information Commons Governance Group works together to pool funds to acquire the needed resources. The Information Commons Governance Group is comprised of library and UITS managers and administrators, and is chaired by the head of the Information Commons Undergraduate Services department.

Publicity/Promotion

The IUB libraries and University Information Technology Services have not focused heavily on promoting the IC. The undergraduate library received 1.2 million visitors the year prior to the opening of the Information Commons. In the 2004 to 2005 fiscal year, the IU IC received 1.9 million visitors. The general assumption is that students liked and used the space before, and the renovation made it even more popular.

Evaluation

Both the IUB Libraries and University Information Technology Services collect interaction statistics and look to the gate counts as a measure of use. The Information Commons Governance Group has surveyed students in the IC using both paper and electronic surveys. In fall 2005, the group conducted regular focus groups and IC user surveys to identify user needs and assess user satisfaction.

◆

KANSAS STATE UNIVERSITY
HALE LIBRARY
MANHATTAN, KANSAS, USA

Total student enrollment: 23,151
Carnegie classification: Doctoral research institution

Date established: 2001
Name: K-State InfoCommons
Square footage of the information commons area: 400,000 square feet
Total square footage of the building: 400,000 square feet
Location: Main library, all floors
Typical access hours per week: 108
Typical service hours per week: 83
Number of service points: 11
Number of computers available for use: Main library: 213 workstations located throughout the library building, plus a wireless network; Weigel Architecture Library: 4 workstations
Average monthly door count: 94,846
Average monthly service transactions: 7,750
Workstation sessions/logins: 27,146
Relevant URLs:
Infocommons website: http://infocommons.k-state.edu/
Software: http://lan.cns.ksu.edu/labs/software/software.htm

Purpose

Students requested access to computing resources along with library resources to enhance writing papers and preparing other academic projects. K-State does not require students to own their own computers, so the university must provide accommodations. The library believes it is important to combine technology and library resources together to encourage students to develop information literacy and to learn the best methods of locating information in a variety of formats.

Services

Separate service points exist for reference and technology help; both are located in the main library. Assistance is available in person, by phone, e-mail, and "chat" for both. The information technology help desk was created along with the InfoCommons. A higher-end computing center, called the Media Development Center, constituted the third phase of the InfoCommmons; it is also housed in the main library. Students can come to several service points throughout the library and be referred to the location best able to offer assistance.

Software

Applications include Microsoft Office, course- and discipline-specific applications, library databases, RefWorks, technology programs, translation software, and adaptive technology programs. See URL listed above for updated listings.

Print Resources

The K-State InfoCommons is scattered throughout the main library building with immediate access to all formats of information and their associated service points. Computers are located in all reference areas, throughout the stacks, in Government Publications, Microforms, Special Collections, study carrels, near the Media Collection, and in technology classrooms. Some terminals are "stand up" to encourage specific use to look up call numbers to access the library print collections.

Staff

Library staff and technology help staff are hired and administered through two different budgets, but cooperate and work together in partnership. Rovers from both entities regularly provide assistance throughout the building and staff desks where students can find assistance as needed. Some desks are staffed by student employees, some by library staff, and some by faculty members. Peak hours include weekday evenings, so staffing is particularly concentrated during those times.

Funding/Budget

Both the library and the information technology units provide staff. Software and hardware are funded in part by a student technology fee. Planning and management are handled by a cooperative team of library and information technology administrators.

Publicity/Promotion

At the opening of the InfoCommons, the library held drawings and gave away prizes to students. Increased use of the facility has eliminated any need for

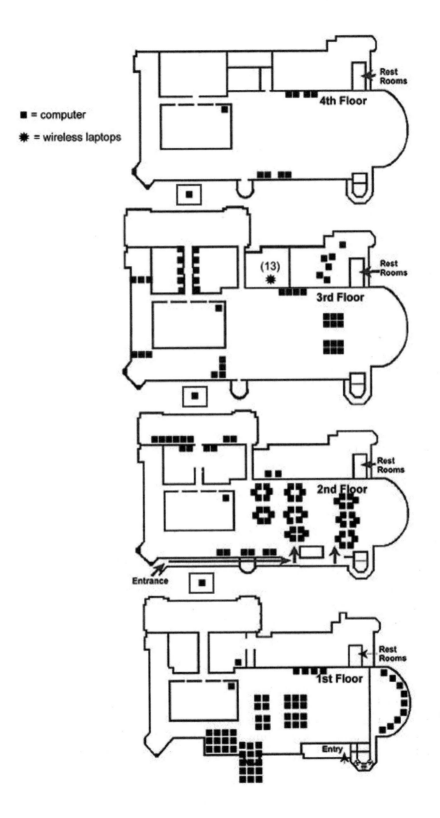

■ = computer

✳ = wireless laptops

4th Floor

Rest Rooms

(13) ✳

3rd Floor

Rest Rooms

2nd Floor

Rest Rooms

Entrance

1st Floor

Rest Rooms

Entry

publicity; library gate counts have increased following the renovation of the building and the introduction of the technology. Informative websites that help students find information about technology offerings are very important and are the best means of educating them about services.

Evaluation

Usability testing of the computer image and associated websites is done annually, with significant upgrades during the summer, and more minor adjustments throughout the academic year. Ongoing communication enables those staffing the library and technology service points to troubleshoot complaints and problems throughout the year.

◆

KENT STATE UNIVERSITY
MAIN LIBRARY
KENT, OHIO, USA

Total student enrollment: 24,000 (Kent campus)
Carnegie classification: Doctoral research institution
Date established: 2003
Name: Information Commons (formal), InfoCommons (colloquial)
Square footage of the information commons area: 26,875 square feet
Square footage of the building: 242,254 square feet assigned to the library (there are other units housed in the building in addition to the library)
Location: Main library; entrance floor and second floor, one space shared with other campus organizations
Typical access hours per week: 99
Typical service hours per week: 77
Number of service points: 4
Number of computers available for use: 130
Average monthly door count: Not available
Average monthly service transactions: Reference, 3,589; Student Multimedia Studio, 803
Workstation sessions/logins: Not available
Relevant URLs:
Information Commons website: www.library.kent.edu/page/10736

Purpose

The purpose is to create an integrated facility for students in the main library that will highlight available knowledge resources, support use of various information technologies, and provide specialized assistance. The Information Commons was seen as a means of providing a focal point to highlight the role the library (and its staff) can play as a teaching-learning center in the digital age.

Services

Reference desk services were retained; periodical information continued as before. Added services include assistance with basic multimedia applications (scanning, image manipulation). The Computer Lab continued, with strengthened communication between library staff and the staff running the lab and the lab help desk. The Group Instruction Lab (seven workstations), an existing facility, was refitted. ADA stations already existed.

Math tutoring is a new service offered in the library as an expansion of tutoring services already offered by the Academic Success Unit. Writing tutoring, another new service in the library, is offered through the combined efforts of the Academic Success Unit and the Writing Center. The GIS workstation was added, as were color printing and color photocopying.

The Student Multimedia Studio was relocated from the third floor and expanded. A new quiet study area, with seating for sixty-six students, was created, along with other casual seating areas. Four existing group study rooms were also refitted. A coffee bar and a second-floor student lounge were added.

Software

All workstations, except those in the large Computer Lab, are managed by the library's system staff. University Information Services manages the lab. Software on computers in the reference area include Microsoft Internet Explorer, Roxio, Netscape, and Notepad. ADA workstations have Zoomtext, Jaws, Narrator, Magnifier, and Microsoft Internet Explorer. Express multimedia stations include Adobe Acrobat, Microsoft Internet Explorer, Microsoft Publisher, Netscape, WS-FTP LE, Photoshop, Roxio, SSH, Paintshop, Epson Scanning Software, and Notepad. The GIS station has ArcView and ArcGIS, Census 2000 longform, Microsoft Office, and Roxio. The Student Multimedia Studio computers have Microsoft Office, Adobe Photoshop, Macromedia Dreamweaver, Netscape Composer, Macromedia Flash, Adobe Acrobat Suite, Adobe Premier, Final Cut Pro, iMovie, Windows Media Encoder, Pinnacle Studio, Sonic Foundry Acid Pro, and Music Studio. In the Computer Lab, stations have Adobe Acrobat Reader, McAfee, Microsoft Internet Explorer, Microsoft FrontPage, Microsoft Office, Microsoft Visual Studio, Netscape Communicator, Quick Time, RealPlayer, Shock Wave, SSH, SPSS, Zip Central, MathLab, and WS-FTP LE.

Print Resources

The library reduced its physical reference collection by half to make room for the components of the Information Commons, and is working to maintain zero-growth in this area. In addition, a very large first floor bibliography collection was sent to storage. The book collection is shelved on floors four through ten. The most used microforms are on the second floor with the current and bound periodicals. Microform equipment has been upgraded and the library now provides scanners that enable users to print to the networked printer.

Staff

The Reference desk is staffed with one librarian and one library science graduate student. Training is provided for the multimedia applications that are avail-

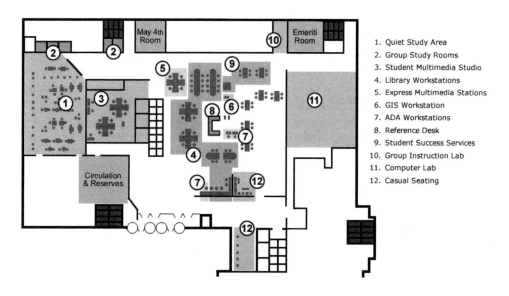

1. Quiet Study Area
2. Group Study Rooms
3. Student Multimedia Studio
4. Library Workstations
5. Express Multimedia Stations
6. GIS Workstation
7. ADA Workstations
8. Reference Desk
9. Student Success Services
10. Group Instruction Lab
11. Computer Lab
12. Casual Seating

able at the express multimedia stations (scanning, image manipulation). The Student Multimedia Studio is staffed with one full-time staff member and student assistants who have backgrounds in areas such as graphic design.

Funding/Budget

Planning for the Information Commons was done by a working group comprised of most members of the Libraries and Media Services management team, the head of Reference Services, and the director of the Student Multimedia Studio. The InfoCommons became a reality from the initial proposal to the grand opening in eight months. One-time funding for construction, furniture, and computers/software came from three sources: Libraries and Media Services, the Provost's Office, and the Chief Information Officer. Daily management is done by the managers of the various service points. Oversight is by the associate dean for Public Services in consultation with the management team as needed.

Publicity/Promotion

The InfoCommons is highlighted in all orientation sessions. The library session of university orientation includes a tour for all freshmen (over 3,000 each year). It is also promoted by liaison librarians with their departments, and through publications, such as the library's newsletter "Footnotes." Its location inside the front doors of the library is probably the best advertisement.

Evaluation

There has not been a formal evaluation; informal feedback has been very positive. Use of the Student Multimedia Studio has skyrocketed 185 percent in two years to over 3,200 student sessions in spring 2005.

◄►

LEHIGH UNIVERSITY
E.W. FAIRCHILD-MARTINDALE LIBRARY
BETHLEHEM, PENNSYLVANIA, USA

Total student enrollment: 5,823 (Spring 2005)
Carnegie classification: Doctoral research institution
Date established: Fall 1997
Name: Information Commons (IC)
Square footage of the information commons area: 9,000 square feet
Square footage of the building: 132,058 square feet
Location: On the main floor, visible from the Library entrance
Typical access hours per week: 118
Typical service hours per week: 90
Number of service points: 1
Number of computers available for use: The IC has 26 networked desktop PCs (4 Macs, 22 PCs). There are another 10 PCs on the south end of the same floor,

and network jacks for users with laptops who wish to connect to the network. Nineteen wireless laptops are available for checkout at the circulation desk nearby. The entire floor is wireless-enabled.

Average monthly door count: 77,229 per month (2004–2005)

Average monthly service transactions: 1,238 per month (2004–2005; includes chat reference and e-mail reference)

Workstation sessions/logins: 7,967 (Spring 2005)

Relevant URLs: Not available

Purpose

The Information Commons (IC) provides a collaborative learning work space for students, with access to state-of-the-art technologies and proximity to library and technology support/service. The Commons offers high-end workstations, scanners, printers, a high-speed network, general and specialized software, and a wide range of research databases and traditional library resources. Lehigh's integrated service model is a distinguishing feature of Lehigh's IC implementation. Library and computing specialists work together at the help desk to assist students with problems that range from starting a research project to troubleshooting a wireless connection. In-depth consulting service is also available during high-volume hours. The overarching goal of the Commons area is to provide students with facilities and resources for technology-focused learning in a supportive environment.

Services

The development of the IC was part of a broad reorganization of Lehigh's library and computing services. In 1997, a merger of the libraries and computing center formed what is now called Library and Technology Services (LTS). As part of this transformation, the reference desk was converted to an integrated computing and library help desk staffed jointly by library and computing support staff. A second-tier consulting office was created for in-depth assistance. In addition to these new service points, the physical facilities were enhanced with more public PCs, a redefined reference/index area, and new seating. Over time, the computing spaces have transitioned from banks of computers to more group-friendly PC/seating arrangements.

The Information Commons now features networked Macs and PCs, networked printing, networked file storage, scanning, kiosks for non-Lehigh visitors, CD-ROM databases, and the reference collection. In the IC (and at all public sites), over 100 commercial software products, and over 100 research databases (including e-journals and full-text) are available. Recent upgrades to IC service include 100 mbps connections to a gigabit-per-second campus backbone, wireless access points, a laptop borrowing service, chat reference, and problem-tracking software that aids staff in tracking problems and communicating progress to clients.

Software

Standard applications, such as Microsoft Office, antivirus software, and web browsers (e.g., Mozilla) are preloaded on desktops. Over 100 commercial (and some shareware) products are made available to networked PCs on campus, including those in the IC, using a product called Prism. Typical software packages include Adobe Acrobat, AutoCAD, Dreamweaver, Photoshop, EndNote, MathCAD, Mathematica, Maple, Macromedia products, Microsoft specialized products such as Project and Frontpage, Scientific Workplace, Rational Suite Enterprise, ArcView, AutoDesk, Borland products, SciFinder Scholar, and many others. A Prism-like software distribution mechanism is planned for networked Macintoshes. Compliance with license restrictions is ensured through a software application called Keyserver.

Questions and problems with software are generally handled by the help desk staff, with assistance from two software librarians, who are part of LTS, and other software specialists on staff. Unipress Footprints problem-tracking software is available to all LTS staff to aid in referral, problem tracking, and communicating with users. Help desk staff rely heavily on this software tool, as do many other LTS staff. Originally designed for computing support, it has been adapted for tracking and resolving both library and computing questions.

Print Resources

The IC is situated on the main floor of the library, reasonably close to all significant library resources. The reference collection is located within the IC. Circulation and reserves are within view of the IC. With the rise of the Internet, the use

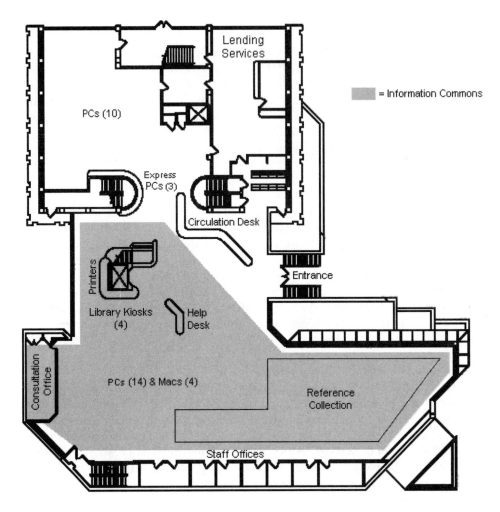

of print reference resources has declined. Reference resources, and indeed most library resources, are purchased or licensed in electronic format when possible. Two PCs equipped with scanners are adjacent to the IC and are designated for library document scanning. A microform scanner is located on the second floor.

Staff

The help desk is staffed by a team of library and computing specialists assigned specifically to support students' research and computing needs (note: residential networking and hardware support are provided by other groups). The team has eight full-time staff members and about twenty student consultants. Help desk staff members currently include two librarians (one librarian is serving as team leader), one senior computing consultant, three computing assistants, and two library assistants. Five librarians not part of the help desk work with the help desk team and staff the IC consulting office.

An important advantage to the Lehigh IC arrangement is that the help desk staff are assigned specifically and permanently to the help desk and, with one exception, all help desk staff reside in offices within the IC area. The team's primary purpose is to develop and enhance computing and library services to students. The investment of full-time staff, and their placement within the IC area, strengthens ownership of the service and team focus.

The desk is staffed as follows: Monday through Thursday, 8 a.m. to 5 p.m., two full-time staff; 5 p.m. to 9 p.m., full-time staff and student; 9 p.m. to 10 p.m., student only. Friday, 8 a.m. to 5 p.m., two full-time staff. Saturday, 10 a.m. to 1 p.m., two students; 1 p.m. to 5 p.m., full-time staff and student. Sunday, 10 a.m. to 1 p.m., two students; 1 p.m. to 9 p.m., full-time staff and student; 9 p.m. to 10 p.m., student.

In recruiting new staff, the library has found it important to look for individuals who are flexible and service oriented. Help desk staff generally have a background in either library work or technology support, but all staff learn basic skills in both areas. Team members frequently refer requests to one another, or to librarian consultants, for support that requires specialized skills.

Funding/Budget

Implementation costs have been estimated at $60,000, including construction of a new help desk, network and power upgrades, upgrading and adding computers, etc. Other aspects of the renovation occurred gradually over time, as funds became available. Equipment upgrades are integrated into life-cycle planning for public computing sites.

Publicity/Promotion

The IC is the busiest, highest-traffic public computing site on campus. The facility's central location, high visibility (at the library entrance), and extended hours of availability (whenever the library is open) make it hard to ignore. A large, colorful, permanent IC banner with an eye-catching graphic is placed above the service desk, which helps to "brand" the area as the IC. Students enjoy the convenience and availability of resources in the IC and proximity to the range of LTS services and support. Services offered within the IC are described and promoted primarily through a help desk website. All LTS bulletins include the tag line "call the help desk with questions," which serves to establish the service point as a center for LTS support. The help desk/IC staff is heavily involved in publicizing news about the library and computing center and developing documentation/instructional guides.

Evaluation

The help desk periodically distributes a user satisfaction survey to assess how well the service is performing in areas such as courtesy and effectiveness in answering questions. Each February, staff track and document all questions received using the Footprints problem-tracking database. Footprints provides a statistical analysis of problems by type and subtype, as well as other dimensions. This analysis assists in determining and addressing the "pain points" of service and in identifying training priorities.

Northwestern University
Northwestern University Library
Evanston, Illinois, USA

Total student enrollment: 15,659
Carnegie classification: Doctoral research institution
Date established: 2004
Name: Information Commons (IC)
Square footage of the information commons area: 5,100 square feet
Square footage of the building: 368,000 square feet
Location: Main library; first floor (main entrance)
Typical access hours per week: 115
Typical service hours per week: 105
Number of service points: 1
Number of computers available for use: 58
Average monthly door count: 56,000
Average monthly service transactions: 1,423
Workstation sessions/logins: 80,040 per month (average for spring quarter, 2005)
Relevant URLs:
Information Commons website: www.library.northwestern.edu/ic/

Purpose

The Information Commons (hereafter IC or Commons) is a joint venture between the library and Northwestern University Information Technology (NUIT)'s Academic Technologies (AT) division. The IC provides a technologically rich and welcoming environment that supports and encourages many of the new practices in scholarship, teaching and learning, and electronic publishing that are part of the digital landscape in higher education. Users draw upon the expertise of Commons staff as they engage in independent inquiry or small-group interactions. They have seamless access to new technologies and research services in zones that are individually focused, yet sufficiently flexible to enable ambient learning and group activities. The Commons thus supports Northwestern University's strong commitment to promoting collaboration across disciplines in order to enable users to enter the research-to-knowledge cycle at any stage. Staff assistance—both technical and informational—is available at the service desk at all times, with referral to other departments as necessary.

In order to encourage group work and collaborative enterprises, furniture in the IC is modular and flexible, which allows for a variety of configurations. A group project room, in which users can develop and practice presentations, is equipped with SMART boards.

Services

Prior to the IC's establishment, the area was known as the General Information Center, with a help desk (staffed by a library staff member and/or a student assistant) and several computers with Internet-only access. Because the IC is a collaborative venture between the library and Academic Technologies, service in the IC includes both an informational component as well as a technological one. The service desk stands alone; it is one of three units in the Reference department, which still maintains a separate reference desk.

Software

All IC computers provide access to the same software available on any public computer in the library, although the IC computers are restricted to Northwestern users only. The software includes a web browser for Internet and e-mail use, as well as access to online databases; the complete suite of Microsoft Office; several general packages such as Ebrary Reader; and more specialized software, such as SciFinder Scholar and Beilstein.

Print Resources

There are no print resources in the IC. Users who require print/microform materials are referred to other departments. The IC is designed to be self-contained, but able to merge smoothly with other units as the need arises. The guiding philosophy behind this approach is that users can begin their work in an environment that is familiar and comfortable to them, where many of the necessary

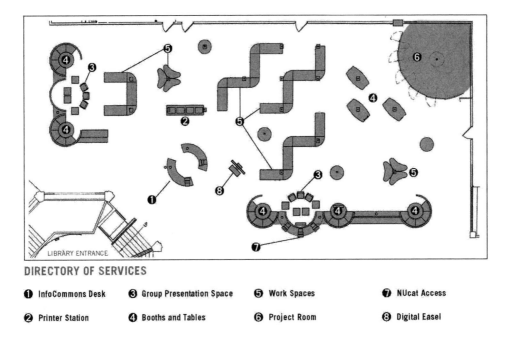

DIRECTORY OF SERVICES

❶ InfoCommons Desk   ❸ Group Presentation Space   ❺ Work Spaces   ❼ NUcat Access

❷ Printer Station   ❹ Booths and Tables   ❻ Project Room   ❽ Digital Easel

resources are available to them online, and where they do not need to leave their workstations or groups in order to produce their work. The proximity to the reference desk and to the Periodicals and Newspapers Reading Room ensures that more specialized research assistance—or additional referral—is available as necessary.

Staff

Two consultants are always on duty at the service desk. AT provides (and pays for) student assistants from their pool of computer lab assistants. The library uses student assistants, full-time staff, and some volunteers; the evening supervisor is a library staff member. Training is conducted throughout the year to ensure that everyone has basic informational and technological skill sets. More specialized skills are handled by separate AT and library training.

Funding/Budget

The IC coordinator is a library staff member, who reports directly to the head of Reference, and has direct responsibility for the day-to-day operations of the IC. Overall management of and planning for the IC is a joint library-AT responsibility, conducted primarily through regular meetings and e-mail. The IC is funded primarily by the library, which also provides half of the staffing: student assistants, volunteers, and staff. AT supplies and pays for student consultants, who assist with technological issues as well as basic informational needs.

Publicity/Promotion

Library orientations emphasize the IC as an area for collaboration and for student work. Information about the IC is sent to the student newspaper, the staff/faculty weekly bulletin, and a newsletter for donors, and is available at various places on both AT and Library web pages.

Evaluation

Three to five times a year, short written surveys are conducted by student assistants for one week during all hours that the IC is open. Students' responses show that 75 percent of them believe the IC met their group project needs through the booths, tables, and collaborative spaces around workstations. Findings also indicate that over 80 percent of surveyed students used the IC on a daily or weekly basis, and students' most common IC activities included e-mailing, and researching and writing papers. Approximately 80 percent of student respondents found the noise level was usually acceptable (cell phones are allowed).

OREGON STATE UNIVERSITY
VALLEY LIBRARY
CORVALLIS, OREGON, USA

Total student enrollment: 19,162 (2004–2005)
Carnegie classification: Doctoral research institution
Date established: 1998
Name: The Valley Library Information Commons (IC)
Square footage of the information commons area: 22,485 square feet
Square footage of the building: 335,087 square feet
Location: Main library, main floor (second)
Typical access hours per week: 111.5
Typical service hours per week: 111.5
Number of service points: 1
Number of computers available for use: 110
Average monthly door count: 96,037 for the entire library
Average monthly service transactions: 3,374
Workstation sessions/logins: 45,000 average logins per month
Relevant URLs:
Information Commons website: http://osulibrary.oregonstate.edu/computing/

Purpose

The Valley Library Information Commons (IC) opened in 1999 following the award-winning remodel of the former Kerr Library to the Valley Library. The original concept for the IC included providing a facility where the typical student could carry an assignment from the conception of an idea and research through

to production. The IC was designed to offer access to library resources, hardware and software tools, and on-site expert help, such as reference and technical assistance. The services and technology offerings in the newly created Information Commons were based on surveys of the anticipated needs and desires of representative samples of faculty, students, and departmental representatives. Individuals from the local public school system were also interviewed about the typical technical skills of graduating seniors. The 2004 opening of the Collaborative Learning Center (CLC), located adjacent to the Information Commons, further expanded the original IC concept to include directed study tables, tutoring, and study assistance.

To facilitate both individual and collaborative research and study, the IC design includes tables, lounge seating, and individual computer carrels. A study room was set aside to enable group viewing of videos or CDs/DVDs. In addition, individual viewing stations with headphones were provided.

Services

The Information Commons offers a variety of services and resources to OSU students, faculty, staff, and the general public. Reference staff provide in-person, phone, and digital reference services, and individual consultations with subject librarians. New services include student assistants to provide technical support, and a direct phone line to the OSU computer help desk. When the IC opened, the OSU Writing Center, the Career Center, and other departments on campus began offering tutoring and study assistance using peer tutors and graduate teaching assistants. Those services are now located in the CLC.

Before the IC opened, students had access only to library resources and limited access to the Internet. One hundred and ten computer workstations now allow access to digital resources, including databases, production software, e-mail, color and black-and-white printing, scanning, and photocopying. Laptop computers can be checked out from the circulation desk (on the same floor) to take advantage of the wireless network throughout the building. Most study tables are wired for computer use. To accommodate persons with disabilities, adaptive equipment and workstations are provided. Study tables, lounge seating, individual computer carrels, video and CD/DVD viewing stations, and a group viewing room are also available.

Software

The library offers numerous software packages that enable patrons to access library collections and electronic resources, as well as office productivity resources students need to synthesize the information they gather into multimedia class presentations or research projects.

The computers in the Information Commons area are all loaded with the following software: Adobe Reader, AlternaTIF, DjVe for Internet Explorer, Ebrary Reader, Foxfire, Flash plug-in, Ghost Script, Ghost View, IBM Homepage Reader, Internet Explorer, InterVideo WinDVD 2000, Java plug-in, Microsoft Office 2003, Norton Antivirus, QuickTime, Roxio CD Burning, Shockwave plug-in, and Windows Media Player. The Microsoft Office applications are only available to students who log in to the system with their OSU Identification Number (ONID).

In addition to the computer workstations above, the IC has one adaptive PC that includes a Pentium with 3.5 MB RAM, 18″ LCD Monitor, ZIP250 and Windows XP SP1 operating system. The software loaded on the computer includes Dragon Naturally Speaking, IBM Homepage Reader, Jaws, Kurzweil 3000, Omnipage, Openbook, Supernova, and Triangle. There is also access to an Aladdin Genie Computer Interface CCTV and a scanner with automatic document feeder, as well as a Braille printer.

Print Resources

The Information Commons is adjacent to the print reference collection and on the same floor as the current newspaper collection. The remainder of the library's print collections are located on the other five floors of the building and in off-site storage. Reserve materials are available from the Circulation Desk. Microforms and microform printers are located on the third floor of the library near the University Archives, one floor above the Information Commons, as are the maps and government publications. These materials are co-located to facilitate use.

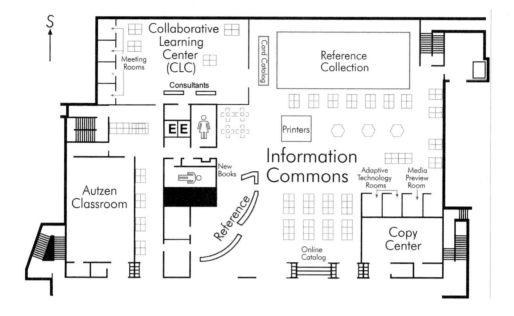

Staff

The Reference and Instruction department staffs the Information Commons centralized reference and information desk with professional librarians, on-call (substitute) librarians, classified staff, library school interns, and student assistants. Student workers answer directional questions and assist with technical issues, while the rest of the staff is responsible for reference queries. The IC is staffed during all library open hours. The level of staffing varies throughout the day, from a single student assistant to two students and two other library staff, depending on when the heaviest use is anticipated. Most of the reference and instruction librarians are required to work at the reference desk during regular day shifts, and some evenings and weekends. In addition, all reference staff, except for students, are responsible for digital reference services. The librarians share responsibility for coordinating the reference operations through a weekly rotation as "duty officer."

All reference staff and students receive extensive training based on training materials developed by the reference operations work group before they can work alone on the desk. Classified staff receive the same training as professional librarians. Student workers are recruited through the university's career service center.

Funding/Budget

Initial funding for the Information Commons came from student contributions to the library's remodeling funds. Ongoing funding for equipment is acquired through the university's technology resource funds, gift money, and the general operations budget. Funding for the rest of the IC services and staffing comes from the Reference and Instruction, and Library Technology budgets.

Planning and management for the facility is chiefly the responsibility of the Reference and Instruction department, in consultation with the associate university librarian for Public Services and the library director. Changes in services are coordinated with other Public Services departments.

Publicity/Promotion

The IC participates in annual academic year kickoff events held on campus, and sponsors activities during this time that draw students into the library. As new equipment or services are added, they are promoted in the student and university newspapers and, on occasion, in the local community newspapers. Existing services are highlighted throughout the academic year in these same venues. Librarians also advise students on use of the IC and CLC during instructional sessions.

Evaluation

Following the opening of the IC, students were surveyed to determine how they were using the new facility. OSU libraries have participated in three LibQual assessments and questions concerning the IC were inserted into each of the surveys. In 2005, the OSU Business and Research offices conducted a year-long study of library use to determine cost-per-use averages. Other than gathering usage statistics, no other ongoing data gathering has occurred. A user satisfaction assessment is planned for this academic year.

◆

SIMON FRASER UNIVERSITY
W.A.C. BENNETT LIBRARY
BURNABY, BRITISH COLUMBIA, CANADA

Total student enrollment: 19,345
Carnegie classification: Doctoral research institution
Date established: 2003
Name: Alumni Information Commons (IC or Info Commons)
Square footage of the information commons area: 15,000 square feet
Square footage of the building: approximately 280,000 square feet
Location: Main library, main floor
Typical access hours per week: 100
Typical service hours per week: 70
Number of service points: 1
Number of computers available for use: 179 stations (144 PCs, 35 Macs)
Average monthly door count: 200,000 during peak months
Average monthly service transactions: 4,000 during peak months
Workstation sessions/logins: Not available

Relevant URLs:

Information Commons website: www.info-commons.sfu.ca/

Simon Fraser news announcement: www.sfu.ca/advancement/alumni_giving/
   Info_Commons.html

Purpose

For many years, the W.A.C. Bennett Library housed a general drop-in computing lab on the second floor known as the "Wordstation." This drop-in facility was
administered by the university's Academic Computing Services (ACS).

As library resources became available electronically, the Bennett Library continued to add computing workstations within the building to access licensed
electronic resources. These library workstations did not provide students with
productivity software. In time, demand for multipurpose workstations increased,
with frequent lines for library and Wordstation computers. At certain times of
the year, some library workstations sat unused while students lined up for the
Wordstation.

In late 2002, the university librarian and the director of Academic Computing
Services proposed relocating the Wordstation to the main floor of the library,
adding student technicians to the reference desk in order to create an information
commons facility where students could conduct library research as well as create
scholarly material with productivity software (such as Microsoft Word, Excel, and
PowerPoint). With support from the university, the library, and the Alumni En-

dowment Fund, the Alumni Information Commons officially opened in fall 2003. Its motto is "collaborative, innovative, integrated."

Services

Before the Information Commons opened, students with questions about computing or software had to contact the ACS help desk, which was physically located in another building. A direct telephone line was available from a phone on the wall of the Wordstation. With the creation of the Information Commons, Academic Computing Services agreed to provide a student technician—often referred to as an IC technician—within the library.

The Bennett reference desk, which had three librarian stations, was transformed into the SFU Alumni Information Commons service desk. A fourth station was created for the IC technician. The Alumni Information Commons service desk is a single, integrated desk where students and faculty can approach staff for library research and technical assistance. Friendly referrals to the appropriate staff take place regularly.

Software

Software on the Information Commons computers includes Acrobat Reader 6, Crimson Editor 3.51, GS View 2.9, GhostScript 6.01, FirstClass, Microsoft Office 2003 (Word, Excel, PowerPoint, Access, Photo Editor), QuickTime 6, RealOne Player, Windows Media Player 9, Internet Explorer 6, SSH Telnet Client 3.0, Mozilla, JMP In 4, Maple 8, MiniTab 13, S-Plus 6.1, SPSS 11.5, SysStat 10.2, SAS v.8, Norton AntiVirus, and WinRAR (not available on the Macs).

ACS and the Library Systems staff cooperate to determine what to include in the download for each computer. Each unit is responsible for troubleshooting technical issues on the computers that they lease, but they communicate with each other on a regular basis. The majority of IC computers are leased and administered by ACS. Some of the Information Commons computers on the main floor are leased and administered by Library Systems, which is also responsible for computers on other floors. With few exceptions, almost all public library workstations in the Bennett Library have the same functionality as the Information Commons computers.

Print Resources

The reference collection was significantly weeded to make room for the Information Commons. The print indexes were also relocated to the second floor (where the Wordstation used to be). The working reference collection is located on the same floor as the IC service desk. Books and journals are located on other floors of the library.

Staff

Librarian stations at the IC desk are staffed by continuing professional librarians and senior reference assistants. The reference division also hires temporary librarians for short-term contracts for evening and weekend coverage. The IC

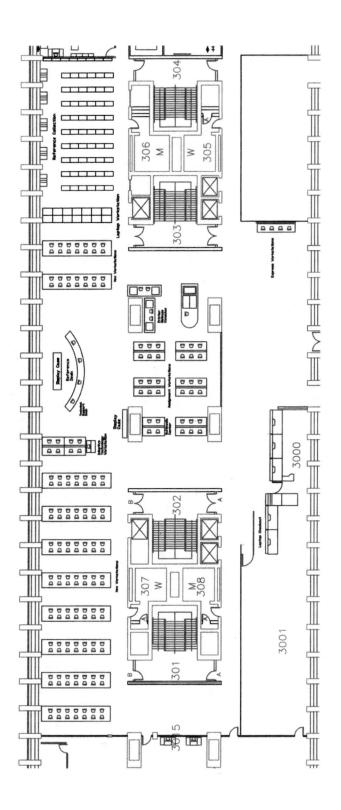

desk is staffed by one to three librarians, with a maximum of three librarians at the busiest times during the regular term.

The IC technician's station is staffed by students hired and trained entirely by ACS. ACS attempts to match librarians' service hours as closely as possible. During the regular term (September through April) the IC desk is open Monday through Thursday, 9 a.m. to 8 p.m.; Friday, 9 a.m. to 6 p.m.; and Saturday and Sunday, 10 a.m. to 6 p.m.

Funding/Budget

The university provided designated funds for the setup and operation of the Information Commons, as did the SFU Alumni Association; other money was found in the library budget. The IC is now fully integrated into the library's ongoing budget and planning.

Each semester, the associate university librarian for Public Services (Bennett Library) chairs a meeting for all IC stakeholders from the library and Academic Computing Services (e.g., librarians, technicians, and managers from the Systems, Facilities, and Reference departments and their counterparts from ACS) to discuss plans and issues. Service provision, software implementation, and technical troubleshooting proceed along established channels among these stakeholders on an ongoing basis.

Publicity/Promotion

An Information Commons web page (see above) is linked from the library and ACS homepages. The "grand opening" in September 2003 received coverage in *SF News* (see link above), and notices for the new facility were also placed in this newsletter. The biggest advertisement happens every day, as hundreds of students pour into the library to access computers for a wide variety of information and social needs. The Information Commons is front and center as they enter the building.

Evaluation

No formal evaluation of this facility has taken place to date. Questions about the IC were included in the last library user survey, conducted in November 2003. At that point, 58 percent of student respondents indicated that they had used the Information Commons facility and found it useful.

◆

St. Martin's University
O'Grady Library
Lacey, Washington, USA

Total student enrollment: 1,126
Carnegie classification: Master's college or university

Date established: 2001
Name: Information Commons
Square footage of information commons area: 3,600 square feet
Square footage of building: 43,000 square feet (3 floors)
Location: Main library, main floor
Typical access hours per week: 85
Typical service hours per week: 85
Number of service points: 1
Number of computers available for use: 32 in the Information Commons proper; an
  additional 22 public computers elsewhere; and wireless and Ethernet access in
  the Information Commons and throughout the library for laptop users
Average monthly door count: 30,085 (Fall 2004)
Average monthly service transactions: 890
Workstation sessions/logins: Not available
Relevant URLs: Not available

Purpose

The construction of the O'Grady Library, opened in 2001, was an opportunity
to expand not only library services and resources, but also technology resources
available on campus. Initial plans called for Saint Martin's Integrated Technology
Services (ITS) and the library simply to share the building. It was quickly seen
that this offered new opportunities for closer collaboration. The Information Commons was identified as a particularly promising option: a joint venture between
the library and academic computing, with the goal of blending traditional reference with computer services. Students would be able to consult reference books
and electronic resources, write papers, and manipulate data all in one place, with
both research and technology help readily available.

Services

The Information Commons has a reference desk, and the reference staff is responsible for providing technology support as well as typical reference services.
Except for 8 p.m. to 11 p.m., Monday through Thursday, librarians or paraprofessional staff members serve at the reference desk. During the late evening hours,
a student is responsible for the desk. He or she provides technology support, but
refers users with research-related questions to librarians.
The offices for two reference librarians and the library's technology coordinator are located in the Information Commons; ITS is on the same floor. Additional
support—both in research and technology—is readily available to reference staff
on the desk, at least 8 a.m. to 5 p.m., Monday through Friday.
The reference desk is also the place students submit applications for network
accounts, homepages, and dorm Internet access. They can also pick up software
licensed by the university for most students (Microsoft Campus Agreement), and
they can even purchase network cables. The reference staff in the Information
Commons is an intermediary between students and ITS.

The previous library facility had only about eight computers, which provided access to the catalog, research databases (CD and online), and the Internet; these machines did not have word processing or e-mail access. Those applications were only available in a computer lab—a separate facility in a different building.

Software

All workstations currently run Windows XP and have the full Microsoft Office suite installed, as well as Microsoft Visual Studio and several discipline-specific applications, including MATLAB (mathematics), Inspiration (education), and MINITAB (statistics). Four workstations have Adobe Photoshop Elements and the Macromedia suite of graphics and web development software. Other configurations are found elsewhere in the library: assistive technology stations, scanning stations with graphics applications, and video-editing stations. While these are not physically located in the Information Commons, they are supported by library staff stationed at the reference desk in the Information Commons and by the library's technology coordinator.

All workstations are networked and login requires a campus network account. The network account includes a campus e-mail box and address, storage on the campus file server (when saving to My Documents), and Internet access.

For technology support, users first turn to the reference desk. This includes problems with a network account (the reference staff can reset passwords), printing, or how to format a table in Word. If the staff person on the desk cannot solve the user's problem, the user will be referred to the library's technology coordinator or one of the library's more technology-savvy librarians, who are available Monday through Friday, 8 a.m. to 5 p.m. If the problem is a network issue or some other matter beyond the scope or expertise of the technology coordinator, the reference desk will call the help desk at ITS, which supports academic computing. ITS is also responsible for purchasing and maintaining the hardware and most of the software in the Information Commons.

The library's technology coordinator, who reports to the electronic services librarian, is responsible for coordinating technology support in the Information Commons (and throughout the library), and offers technology training workshops and one-on-one sessions in the applications available. The technology coordinator also creates short technology guides that are published on the library website for use by students, as well as the reference staff. The technology coordinator is the library's primary liaison with ITS.

Print Resources

The reference collection is housed in the Information Commons. Patrons thus have access not only to online resources and computer applications, but also to print resources right at the workstations. Circulating stacks are one floor up, and print journals and microfiche and microfilm are one floor down. Online indexes include links not only to full-text holdings, but also to catalog records for print and microform holdings.

With the Information Commons, both print and online resources are readily available to faculty and students, as are the tools they need to access and use these materials. Most importantly, students and faculty can also find the support and training they need to take full advantage of these information resources and technologies.

Staff

Currently all staff in the Information Commons are library staff. By tradition and policy, all library staff are scheduled at a public service desk; everyone in the library, except for circulation staff, spends several hours a week at the reference desk. Scheduling is handled by the public services librarian.

There are two positions directly tied to the Information Commons. The technology coordinator has a background that includes experience in desktop support, some network support, and teaching technology. The second position, an evening student employee position, was established to provide technology support during those hours when the technology coordinator is not available. All reference staff provide technology support to the best of their ability; most of their training has been on the job.

Funding/Budget

The initial purchase of the computers and furniture for the facilities was part of the building project budget. ITS is responsible for purchasing and replacing PCs

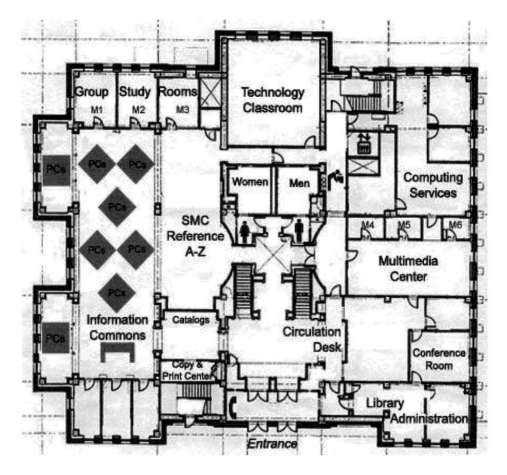

and for software licensing and installation, but the library participates in equipment selection and upgrade planning. There are a few applications that are not part of the typical packages that the library has purchased. Decisions about staffing and hours are made by the library, in consultation with ITS as necessary.

Publicity/Promotion

The initial promotion was part of the new building's grand opening ceremonies. The library is in a prominent location on the campus, and the Information Commons is prominently located just inside the main doors. Most students know where the Information Commons is, but they may not be aware of all the services available. As part of their first-year seminar, all freshmen meet with librarians in the library, and the Information Commons is introduced during their visit.

Evaluation

Several satisfaction surveys conducted since the building and Information Commons opened show a very high level of satisfaction with the technology, information resources, and services provided. The surveys, however, also show that not as many students and faculty are aware of all the services provided in the Information Commons, particularly technology training, which indicates a need for additional marketing of services.

◆

Texas Christian University
Mary Couts Burnett Library
Fort Worth, Texas, USA

Total student enrollment: 8,600
Carnegie classification: Doctoral research institution
Date established: 2002
Name: Information Commons (IC)
Square footage of the information commons area: 12,849 square feet
Square footage of the building: 144,490 square feet
Location: Main library; all services are on one floor
Typical access hours per week: 109
Typical service hours per week: 109
Number of service points: 3
Number of computers available for use: 114 desktop and 30 laptops
Average monthly door count: Not available
Average monthly service transactions: 3,324 calls
Workstation sessions/logins: Not available
Relevant URLs:
Information Commons website: www.ic.tcu.edu/

Purpose

The Information Commons (IC) combines the expertise of reference librarians and campus IT staff to provide integrated support for TCU faculty, staff, and students. Use of information technology and access to information content for both administrative and academic purposes is best supported by an integrated delivery of services.

Services

At the Information Commons service desk, staff include students and full-time employees. Walk-up IC services for tier 1 include student assistance with passwords, network connectivity, and printing services. This tier provides an enhanced number of service hours and staffing beyond what was previously provided by the IT department before its integration with the IC.

Tier 2 includes library reference/research services. The reference desk is part of the IC service desk; there is a reference area staffed by a librarian that is accessible to those students who require research assistance. Second tier services also include IT help desk support (IT technical assistance from a full-time IT employee

in a designated area at the IC). Librarians now have night and weekend support on-site by IT staff.

The Information Commons manages "Frog Pods," a special facility for group and collaborative computing that includes PC and Mac computers, mobile and fixed whiteboards, oversized monitors, moveable furniture, wireless keyboards and mice, and sound masking. Use is by reservation. In addition, students have access to thirty laptops for building use.

Tier 3 IC service is offered by both reference and IT staff by appointment. These sessions provide in-depth support for individuals with extensive technical support issues or research projects.

While not physically part of the walk-up service desk, the IC phone center is located within the IC near the service desk. IC computer lab support is available from full-time employees and students who provide assistance with Microsoft Office and other productivity software, Internet access, the library OPAC and other electronic resources, the campus network, and e-mail. Staff and students from the TCU Center for Writing provide assistance at the Writing Center in the Information Commons.

Software

All PCs in the IC computer lab run Microsoft XP Professional software and include Microsoft Office, Adobe Acrobat Reader, AutoCAD, Code Warrior,

MDL CrossFire Commander, Microsoft Internet Explorer, Microsoft Front Page, Mozilla Firefox, Roxio Easy CD Creator, SPSS, SAS, and WS_FTP. The Macintosh computers have Adobe Creative Suite (Photoshop, InDesign, Illustrator, and ImageReady), Genuine Fractals, Dreamweaver, Adobe Acrobat Reader, Fetch, Microsoft Office, Safari, and StuffIt Expander. TCU maintains the current versions of these software packages in the lab.

Print Resources

There are approximately 100 linear feet of ready reference books within a five-foot reach of the staff. These books serve as additional backup to computer reference when online resources are unavailable or are more cumbersome. They are checked out for building use only. Encyclopedias, biographical works, and indices are available for quick perusal as part of a larger reference collection in the IC area. Microform materials are not kept in the IC, but are located across the lobby in the periodicals section; IC staff has basic training in their use for occasions when the periodicals section is not staffed. IC staff will also retrieve books from the interlibrary loan department when needed.

Staff

The IC service desk includes two tiers of staff: student and employee. Students provide the first tier of service, and the second tier is provided by reference librarians, IT employees, and library systems employees. All levels of employees are available 80 of the 109 service hours. Students and employees provide roving assistance as needed. Both the library and the IT department provide training. IT staff have BS degrees and are industry certified; librarians have MLS degrees and on-the-job training. Monthly update training sessions are scheduled year-round for all employees and students. The third tier of service is offered by reference and IT staff by appointment.

Funding/Budget

Management of the Information Commons is a joint responsibility between the dean of the library and the assistant provost for Information Services (CIO). Each department hires and budgets for its employees with advisory input from the other department. Funding for hardware is largely provided by the IT department as part of the ongoing campus technology upgrades. Monthly management meetings address issues, expenses, and concerns with joint support from both departments.

Publicity/Promotion

Both departments promote the Information Commons to newly hired faculty at the New Faculty Fair. An Information Commons website has links to further resources at the campus IT website and the campus library website. The Information Commons is included in TCU campus tours for prospective and new students.

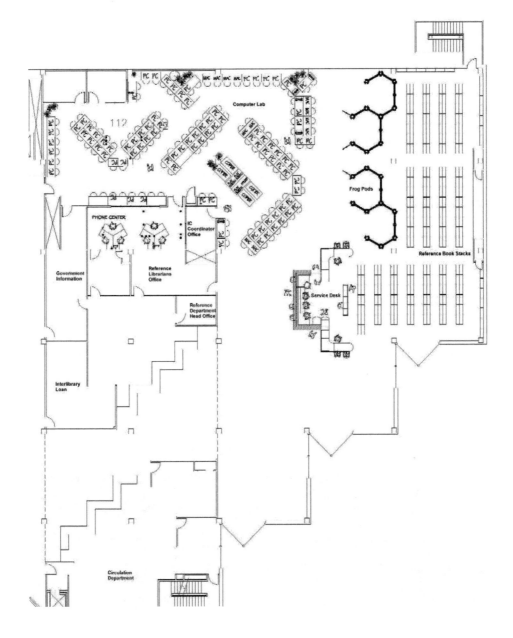

Evaluation

Annual or biannual student web surveys of the Information Commons take place as part of a larger campus commitment to assessment. Recent IC staff surveys provided helpful feedback to administrators who were reviewing current services and planning for future services. A half-day IC staff retreat brought all employees and administrators together to review the Information Commons' successes and future challenges.

◆

Trinity University
Elizabeth Huth Coates Library
San Antonio, Texas, USA

Total student enrollment: 2,718
Carnegie classification: Master's college or university
Date established: 2003
Name: Information Commons (InfoCommons)
Square footage of the information commons area: 20,500 square feet
Square footage of the building: 164,300 square feet
Location: Main library, entrance floor
Typical access hours per week: 96
Typical service hours per week: 96
Number of service points: 1
Number of computers available for use: 95
Average monthly door count: 34,000
Average monthly service transactions: 1,800
Workstation sessions/logins: Not available
Relevant URLs:
InformationCommonswebsite:http://lib.trinity.edu/libinfo/infocommons/index
.shtml

Purpose

The goal for the project was to provide a space that would put the library back
at the intellectual center of the campus. The InfoCommons created academic social

space for students who wished to benefit from the experience of group and collaborative study by emphasizing the value of the library as a place to develop and strengthen students' information literacy skills. The InfoCommons brought together library and IT assistance in one location, and provided a one-stop place for help.

Services

The existing reference service was augmented by staff (mostly students) from IT services. The latter provided a walk-up center at the help desk for IT assistance, something not previously emphasized on campus. The new desk is staffed by both reference and IT staff simultaneously; management remains split between the two administrative units. In addition, a campus copy service run by Kinko's is part of the InfoCommons, and an adjoining coffee shop was nearly doubled in size. In fall 2005, the campus writing center moved into this facility as well.

Software

All computers include Microsoft Office, common campus computer lab packages (statistical, image, language software, etc.), and special library-related software connected to library databases, such as ARTstor Offline Viewer, ArcView, and SciFinder Scholar. Except for the library packages, support is provided by IT staff. IT staff members ask for faculty and library input on what should be loaded on these computers each semester; IT staff then create a common image.

Print Resources

The design intentionally intersperses reference bookshelves around and throughout the InfoCommons, as well as reading stations without computers. The goal is to remind students that useful print sources continue to coexist with those that are accessible by computer. The area is designed in a living-room style, with a comfortable seating area between the two sections of the InfoCommons. The newest book and media acquisitions are placed in that area for browsing.

Staff

Reference staff consists of a group of librarians and library assistants, with four student workers who cover the late and weekend hours. These students are paid from institutional funds, not federal work-study funds, in order to ensure their reliability. IT services provide mostly student workers to cover all hours, along with one part-time staff member. Trinity's InfoCommons does not employ rovers; students doing e-mail, chat, and other personal activities do not appear to appreciate staff wandering immediately behind their workstations. However, both the help desk and reference librarians' offices are sited within the Commons and provide visibility for services.

In fall 2005, the writing center moved into the Information Commons. This service is staffed by two or more students trained and supervised by the English department.

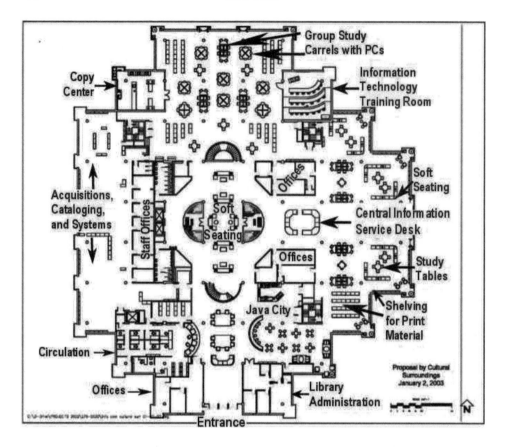

Funding/Budget

Funding for the Information Commons' creation came largely from a generous grant by the Robert Priddy Foundation. Additional computers, added after a few months, were funded from the regular IT budget.

Publicity/Promotion

As the location with the heaviest computer use on campus, the area needs little publicity. There is an InfoCommons website, and the facility and its staff are routinely introduced on tours and during orientation activities. Library instruction largely takes place in a training room that is part of the InfoCommons. The variety of services are featured in the semiannual library newsletter, and campus public relations staff have run announcements and published alumni magazine articles.

Evaluation

The facility has been evaluated largely from use statistics. The first year of the InfoCommons' existence, the library door count increased 15 percent, use of electronic resources rose over 50 percent, and traditional circulation went up 2 percent. Moreover, word-of-mouth from users has been extremely positive. Suggestions for improvement are considered seriously.

◀▬

University of Arizona
Main Library
Tucson, Arizona, USA

Total student enrollment: 36,932
Carnegie classification: Doctoral research institution
Date established: 2002
Name: Information Commons formally, IC or ILC informally
Square footage of the information commons: 29,000 square feet
Square footage of the building: Main library (252,370 square feet) and Integrated Learning Center (54,212 square feet)
Location: On the bottom floor of the main library
Typical access hours per week: 142
Typical service hours per week: 142
Number of service points: 1
Number of computers available for use: 250, with 50 more available in an attached electronic classroom that can be used for overflow
Average monthly door count: Not available
Average monthly service transactions: 4,018
Workstation sessions/logins: Not available
Relevant URLs:
Information Commons website: www.library.arizona.edu/ic/index.html

Purpose

The Information Commons was designed to be a collaborative active learning environment and is part of both the main library and the Integrated Learning Center, which houses classrooms, the University School (academic home of undeclared majors), Equipment Services, and the Digital Media Resource Center. The IC was intended to be both an extension of the classroom and a community in itself where students interact with other students, instructors, librarians, tutors, and technology assistants.

Services

Both reference and technical assistance are provided at a single service point. Neither service was new to the library, but technical assistance was increased significantly as the number of available computers increased. Multimedia Zone staff offer technical assistance for high-end multimedia applications from their offices. Tutoring and writing assistance is offered during selected hours in group study rooms.

Software

For a list of available software, see: www.library.arizona.edu/ic/infocommons-software.html

Print Resources

There is a small reference collection in close proximity to the service point; a larger reference/research collection is located one floor above the IC.

Staff

The service desk is staffed by two librarians/staff and two students between 9 a.m. and 6 p.m., Monday through Friday. From 6 p.m. to 9 a.m. and on weekends, the service desk is staffed by two classified staff and two students.

All employees who work at the service desk go through extensive training that includes reference, customer service, and software support modules. Technical staff support the desktop computers and the servers that support the IC. All staff are library employees.

Funding/Budget

Funding is available from accounts in both the main library and the Integrated Learning Center. The Integrated Learning Center is managed collaboratively by

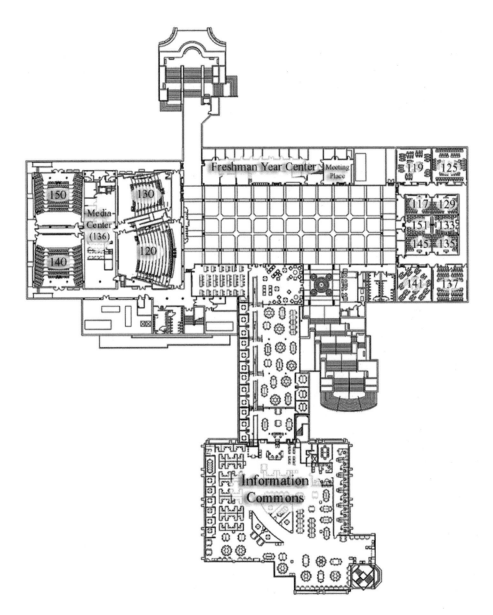

the library, the University School, the University Teaching Center, and the Office of Student Computing Resources.

Publicity/Promotion

When the Information Commons first opened, an advertisement was taken out in the campus newspaper. Since then, no marketing has been required. The facility promotes itself and is full to overflowing most hours of the day. It is featured as part of freshman and transfer student orientation, as well as in spring recruitment tours.

Evaluation

Satisfaction surveys were used the first two years the IC was open. In the last two years the library has conducted an "action gap survey" in order to determine what users want from the facility, what services meet their needs, and what services need improvement.

◀━━

University of Auckland
Grafton Medical and Health Sciences Campus
Faculty of Medical and Health Sciences Building
Auckland, New Zealand

Grafton Medical and Health Sciences Campus Enrollment: 2,766
Carnegie classification: Doctoral research institution
Date established: 2004
Name: The Grafton Information Commons (Grafton IC)
Square footage of the information commons area: 5,274 square feet
Location: One space in a building shared with other campus organizations
Typical access hours per week: 81.5
Typical service hours per week: 81.5
Number of service points: 1
Number of computers available for use: 106
Average monthly door count: 20,240
Average monthly service transactions: 600
Workstation sessions/logins: 28,496
Relevant URLs:
Grafton Information Commons website:
www.information-commons.auckland.ac.nz/?page=gic_faq
Software: www.information-commons.auckland.ac.nz/?page=software#gic

Purpose

The success of the University of Auckland's Kate Edger Information Commons led to the planning and establishment of the Grafton Information Commons. The Grafton Information Commons project was modeled on the successful outcomes of the Kate Edger IC; its environment and service is an extension of the Kate Edger IC. The Grafton facility is used predominantly by medical and health sciences students, but is open to all University of Auckland students.

Services

The Grafton IC provides a HelpDesk, individual computer workstations, printers, scanners, photocopiers, a group study area, casual seating, and a computer training room. Each study space in the Grafton IC is fully wired, and wireless network access is available throughout the building. The Learning Services de-

partment develops and manages learning support services in the Kate Edger and Grafton Information Commons.

The Grafton IC HelpDesk is managed as an extension of the Kate Edger IC HelpDesk service. IC HelpDesk staff are appointed to the Learning Services department and may be required to work in any area that is part of Learning Services. The IC HelpDesk provides a one-stop shop for information, IT, directional, and general inquiries. The IC HelpDesk service is a joint venture between the University Library and Information Technology Systems and Services (ITSS). The University Library takes responsibility for the day-to-day management of the learning support in the Information Commons. The IT Directorate takes responsibility for desktop support and support of NetAccount, the university's authentication and authorization system.

Software

Selected specialist software, provided by the faculty of medical and health sciences, was added to the standard Kate Edger IC desktop. The student desktop software environment meets general student computing needs and is complementary to specialized faculty or departmental computer labs. Students can retrieve information from library databases, e-journals, and e-books; access course work through the university's learning management system; send e-mail and browse

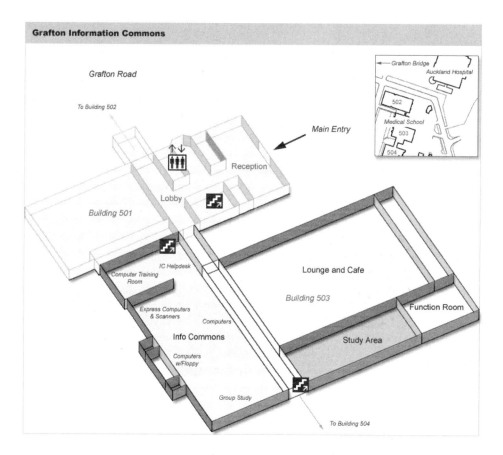

the Internet; and use Microsoft Office and other specialist programs. A full list of software for the Grafton IC is available on the website listed above.

Print Resources

The Philson Medical and Health Sciences Library is located on the level above the Grafton Information Commons and connects to the IC via an internal stairwell.

Staff

Customer service and software support is provided by a member of the Kate Edger IC HelpDesk team. There is normally only one staff member on duty, as the facility is significantly smaller than the Kate Edger IC. Please see the entry on the Kate Edger Information Commons for information on services and support provided by the IC HelpDesk team.

There are no dedicated reference librarians based in the Grafton IC. Medical and health sciences subject librarians use the electronic classroom to deliver information skills courses. The Philson Medical and Health Sciences Library, on the level above the Grafton IC, operates an inquiry desk service.

The IT environment in the Grafton IC is managed and supported by an IT Directorate. Desktop support is provided by three IT staff members based in the Kate Edger IC. A service level agreement between the IT Directorate and the University Library was developed to formalize the partnership and to manage expectations and outcomes. The partnership with the IT Directorate works very satisfactorily and monthly meetings are held to monitor developments and discuss issues.

Funding/Budget

The budget for the Grafton IC is part of the Kate Edger IC budget.

Publicity/Promotion

Notices, posters, pamphlets, websites, and official university publications are used to keep students and faculty informed. A monthly newsletter is published in print and electronic formats. The Grafton Information Commons and associated services are also marketed in the university prospectus, departmental handbooks, and other official publications, as well as in talks during orientation.

Evaluation

Students can use an electronic suggestions box on the Kate Edger Information Commons website to ask questions and to provide feedback. The facility and services will be evaluated in an upcoming library customer satisfaction survey.

◆

UNIVERSITY OF AUCKLAND
KATE EDGER INFORMATION COMMONS
CITY CAMPUS, AUCKLAND, NEW ZEALAND

Total student enrollment: 31,223
Carnegie classification: Doctoral research institution
Date established: 2003
Name: The Kate Edger Information Commons
Square footage of the information commons area: 73,700 square feet
Square footage of the building: 123,161 square feet
Location: Kate Edger Information Commons is in close proximity to the General Library.
Typical access hours per week: 113
Typical service hours per week: 113
Number of service points: 2
Number of computers available for use: 498 fixed desktop computers and 20 wireless laptops available for borrowing
Average monthly door count: 315,720
Average monthly service transactions: 4,000
Workstation sessions/logins: 185,491

Relevant URLs:
Kate Edger Information Commons website:
www.information-commons.auckland.ac.nz/?page=keic_faq
Software: www.information-commons.auckland.ac.nz/?page=software

Purpose

The University of Auckland needed to increase the amount of study space available in the central area of the City Campus because the libraries were overcrowded and the ratio of study space to students was out of alignment with that in similar institutions. In addition, the impact of student-centered teaching methods, such as problem-based learning, evidence-based learning, reflective study, and group work, had resulted in a growing need for more flexible learning spaces. Learning support services for students were located in different buildings on campus, and it was seen as desirable to locate them in the same building. The Kate Edger Information Commons includes group work areas, private study spaces, open consultation, and adaptable service points that allow a greater tolerance of noise and activity. It has over 1,200 study and casual seats, including about 500 multipurpose computers. Each study space is fully wired, and wireless network access is available throughout the building. The main purpose of the Information Commons is to provide an integrated learning environment where students have access to electronic information resources along with appropriate support.

Services

A strategic realignment of library services and resources in 2000 and 2001 resulted in the creation of the University Library's Learning Services department. This department develops and manages learning support services in the Kate Edger and Grafton Information Commons; coordinates information literacy training across the library system; and develops the library's information literacy initiatives in partnership with faculty, the Student Learning Centre, the Centre for Flexible and Distance Learning, and the IT Directorate. Learning Services teams for the IC HelpDesk service, Information Skills, Short Loan, Foundation Studies, and English Language Self-Access Centre (ELSAC) are located in the Kate Edger IC. The substantial size of the facility created the opportunity to co-locate many of these learning support services.

The IC HelpDesk, a new service providing a one-stop shop for information, IT, directional, and general inquiries, was created by merging the IT Directorate's Electronic Campus Help Desk with the University Library's Learning Services. The IC HelpDesk service is a joint venture between the University Library and Information Technology Systems and Services (ITSS); the University Library takes responsibility for day-to-day management of the walk-in and roving support in the Information Commons, while the IT Directorate is responsible for desktop support and NetAccount, the university's authentication and authorization system.

The IC is also home to the University Library's high-demand print and video collection for arts, science, and business and economics students. The collection consists of over 8,000 prescribed and recommended texts, and is available for short loan or reserve (one- to two-hour loans).

The University Library's Information Skills team works closely with subject librarians across the library system to design, develop, and deliver the library's multifaceted information literacy program, initiatives, and resources. The Kate Edger IC has four electronic classrooms that are used for IT and information literacy teaching.

The English Language Self-Access Centre was transferred to the University Library's Learning Services department as a strategic move to create an integrated and collaborative learning environment in the Kate Edger IC. The ELSAC assists all students from non-English-speaking backgrounds. It supports the growing number of English-as-another-language students at the university in improving their English language skills through guided self-study in an electronic learning environment.

The Student Learning Centre assists undergraduate and postgraduate students in developing learning and performance skills through workshops and individual consultations.

Software

The student desktop software environment meets general student computing needs and is complementary to specialized faculty or departmental computer

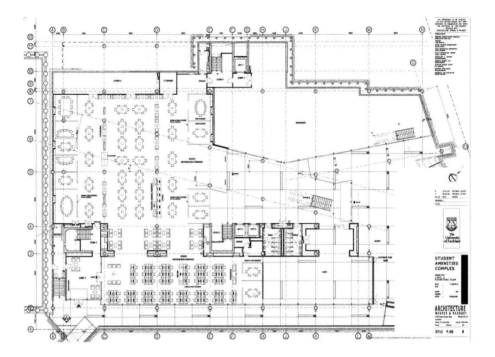

labs. Students can retrieve information from library databases, e-journals, and e-books; access course work through the university's learning management system; send e-mail and browse the Internet; and use Microsoft Office and other specialist programs. A full list of software is available on the website listed above.

Print Resources

The Kate Edger IC differs from many other information commons in that it is a purpose-built facility and is not part of an existing library. The only print collection in the Kate Edger Information Commons is the short-loan collection described above.

Staff

Customer service and software support is provided by the IC HelpDesk team. The team consists of a full-time IC HelpDesk manager, six part-time IC supervisors, and more than thirty part-time IC consultants. The IC consultants are senior students (final year undergraduate or postgraduate) and work a minimum of eight hours per week. The service consists of two components—the IC Help area provides walk-in support to students, NetAccount sales, and open consultation space, while IC consultants provide first-tier roaming support on levels zero, two, three, and four.

IC consultants serve as primary student support staff in the Information Commons. They support students using the computers in the Information Commons, work shifts on the IC HelpDesk, and assist with special projects. They have a general knowledge of electronic resources, software, and databases in the Information Commons, on the campus network, and on the Internet. They are trained in Microsoft Office software, and provide assistance to users in creating documents and spreadsheets, and solving other production-related issues. Group training is provided at the start of each semester and all new recruits receive comprehensive training at the start of their employment.

There are no dedicated reference librarians based at the IC HelpDesk, but subject librarians use the electronic classrooms extensively to deliver information skills courses. The General Library, across the street from the Information Commons, operates an inquiry desk service, and there is close cooperation between the two service points.

The IT environment in the Kate Edger Information Commons is managed and supported by the IT Directorate. Desktop support is provided by three IT staff members who are based in the IC. A service level agreement between the IT Directorate and University Library was developed to formalize the partnership and to manage expectations and outcomes. The partnership with the IT Directorate works very satisfactorily, and monthly meetings are used to monitor developments and discuss issues.

Funding/Budget

The annual recurring operational budget for the Kate Edger Information Commons is NZ$250,858 (approximately $180,000 USD), excluding depreciation, occupancy, staff costs, and equipment leases. The budget for computer leases is NZ$466,287 ($330,000 USD). The library staffing budget for all Learning Services teams, including the IC HelpDesk, is NZ$1,119,780 ($800,000 USD). The budget for the IC HelpDesk team (manager, supervisors, and consultants) is NZ$421,316 ($300,000 USD). The IT Directorate budget for systems support is NZ$150,000 ($105,000).

Publicity/Promotion

The Kate Edger Information Commons is a highly visible new building in the center of the City Campus. Many presentations on the planned IT infrastructure and services were made to faculty before the facility opened. The library operated an Interim Commons for approximately one year before opening the Kate Edger Information Commons, familiarizing students with the types of services and facilities planned for the new IC. Notices, pamphlets, websites, and official university publications were used to keep students and faculty informed.

The Kate Edger Information Commons is the preferred study and social space on the City Campus and consistently has the highest occupancy of all campus library facilities. A monthly newsletter is published in a print and an electronic format. The Kate Edger Information Commons and associated services are also marketed in the university prospectus, departmental handbooks, and other official publications, and in talks during orientation.

Evaluation

The facility and services were rated the highest of all student services and facilities surveyed in the university's biannual first-year undergraduate survey and in the biannual final-year undergraduate survey in 2003. It also rated very highly in the University Library's 2003 customer services survey. Students can use an electronic suggestions box on the Kate Edger Information Commons website to ask questions and to provide feedback.

Interesting trends regarding the use of high-demand material have emerged since the IC opened in 2003. The daily issues (charge outs) of high-demand material increased by 42 percent in 2003 and again by 35 percent in 2004. The trend may be attributed to factors such as a higher visibility of the collection in the Kate Edger Information Commons, open access that allows students to browse and find other relevant books, information skills courses that increase awareness of available resources, greater awareness of overnight loans, ability to borrow three books at a time, and the self-service function of the book return unit, self-issue machines, and online renewals.

UNIVERSITY OF CALGARY
MACKIMMIE LIBRARY
CALGARY, ALBERTA, CANADA

Total student enrollment: 35,500
Carnegie classification: Doctoral research institution
Date established: 1999
Name: Information Commons or Info Commons or Commons
Square footage of the information commons area: 42,044 square feet
Square footage of the building: 290,628 square feet
Location: Main library, second floor of the library
Typical access hours per week: 148
Typical service hours per week: 148
Number of service points: 3
Number of computers available for use: 230
Average monthly door count: 14,608 average daily count
Average monthly service transactions: 85,000 for 2004–2005
Workstation sessions/logins: Not available
Relevant URLs:
Information Commons website: http://library.ucalgary.ca/infocommons/

Purpose

The Information Commons is an integrated service facility whose vision is to provide the space, technology, and expertise needed to support the scholarly use of information resources and to act as a focal point for information services. Planned goals of the Commons were that the user will acquire information lit-

eracy and information technology skills, acquire information resources, acquire help, and have access to various spaces/technology to complete their work.

Services

The services offered include information/general reference service, technology assistance, instruction in information literacy, instruction in productivity software, and expert consultation services for research and productivity problems. Specialized assistance and software are offered for maps, data, and geographic information. The Information Commons service desk is the one-stop desk from which the user can get both reference and technical assistance. Prior to the opening of the Commons, the library had offered reference service and information literacy instruction; the new Commons introduced an integrated and collaborative service in which the library and information technologies work together to offer one-stop service.

Software

All the workstations are configured with the same software to provide access to the Internet, Microsoft Office suite, and specialized plug-ins. In addition, there is a special media area and an adaptive technology workstation that offer specialized software. There are also seven PCs with specialized software to support maps, academic data, and geographic information (MADGIC) services.

All software and printing are supported by student assistants. Networked laser printers are located throughout the Commons and include five black-and-white printers and one color printer. Users pay for printing by using a swipe card system.

Print Resources

The reference collection is housed in the Information Commons area. Staff direct users to the print, electronic, microform, and other special collections throughout the library.

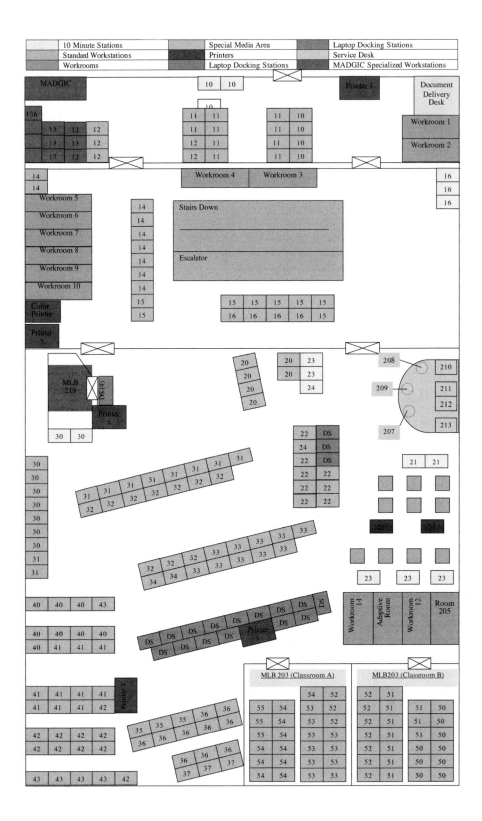

Staff

The staff is a combination of library staff and information technologies staff. The head of the Information Commons directly supervises a support unit (five FTE [full-time employees]), plus a .6 FTE reference librarian and two full-time night assistants for the 24/5 service during fall and winter terms. Information Technologies provides two full-time expert staff (for instruction/consultation and student assistant supervision). Student assistants are hired annually to provide on-the-floor technical assistance. Reference service is provided by a group of thirty librarians and paraprofessionals. The reference group is a mix of subject librarians, support staff, and librarians from units other than subject librarians.

Funding/Budget

The source of the funds is mixed. The library pays for most of the staffing; IT pays for two IT specialists and half of the cost of the student assistants. IT and the library normally share the cost of purchasing new PCs; other equipment, such as printers and scanners, is purchased by the library. Budgeting for the Commons is part of the process of planning for Library Client Services, in collaboration with IT and other units within the library. The head of the Information Commons chairs an operational team comprised of members from the various interested units: Client Services, IT, other Commons in branch libraries, and library technical support. The operational team plans, reviews policies, discusses service issues, and makes recommendations to administration as appropriate.

Publicity/Promotion

The Information Commons and its services are promoted through the annual new student orientation program. Instruction is publicized through the web, classroom handouts, posters, and general announcements. Liaison librarians introduce faculty and students to library services and facilities, including the Information Commons. Commons staff also prepare and distribute pamphlets and brochures in-house, and attend all promotional events on campus.

Evaluation

A web-based evaluation form based on service quality concepts, in use since the Commons opened, invites regular user feedback and allows for tracking of service issues and trends. The library has participated in two LibQual+ surveys in which comments were received regarding the Information Commons. In addition, the Information Commons keeps an hourly count of users of its 24/5 service.

UNIVERSITY OF CAPE TOWN
CHANCELLOR OPPENHEIMER LIBRARY
CAPE TOWN, SOUTH AFRICA

Total student enrollment: 21,300
Carnegie classification: Doctoral research institution

Date established: 2000
Name: The Knowledge Commons (formal); KC (colloquial)
Square footage of the information commons area: 9,140 square feet
Square footage of the building: 136,440 square feet
Location: Main library, at the entrance to the library, occupying one floor of the
    north wing
Typical access hours per week: 74
Typical service hours per week: 74
Number of service points: 1
Number of computers available for use: 105, plus 20 laptops in the training room
Average monthly door count: 48,000
Average monthly service transactions: 7,200
Workstation sessions/logins: 35,000/month
Relevant URLs:
Knowledge Commons website: www.lib.uct.ac.za/kc/

Purpose

By the mid-1990s, the main library was twenty years out of date. The university, with the help of donors, was ready to plan and fund hugely upgraded student development and library facilities. In 1998, a new library director was appointed who brought state-of-the-art ideas with her from the United States.

One of these ideas, the commons, was a totally new concept in South African university libraries.

The Knowledge Commons (KC) was created in 2000 as part of a major retrofit and addition to the university's main library (now the Chancellor Oppenheimer Library). The KC was the first of its kind in Africa, and was inspired by the Leavey Library at the University of Southern California. Its strong customer focus, its high-quality finish, and its innovative staffing have made it a runaway success with students. Most patrons are undergraduates, but a surprisingly high proportion of users are postgraduates.

Services

Before the renovation, the library offered users ten PCs with access to CD-ROM databases, all of which were clustered around one reference desk. Web access and electronic resources were embryonic and usage of the library was poor. With the library's transformation in 2000, there are now three information desks in the main library, with 175 user PCs in the main library alone. Of these, the KC offers 105 PCs, three printers, a scanner, nine group study rooms equipped with PCs, a core collection of reference books, and a training suite with multimedia and twenty laptops. Users who need help with software, with searching for information, or with writing an assignment, can raise a hand, and help is immediately provided by roving staff and student navigators, who are trained and equipped to answer both reference and technical questions.

Software

The KC is operated entirely by library staff. The broader IT infrastructure across the university as a whole is the responsibility of a separate Information and Communication Technology (ICT) department. Printing is an outsourced service.

The software provided is the Microsoft XP Office suite, NetG Skills Builder, and Pharos Uniprint. From the desktop, there are web links to course management software (WebCT and Connect2, which is SAKIA compliant), electronic resources, Aleph (the library catalog), and to the KC sponsor's website. The KC has deliberately avoided specialist software, such as Statistica, SPSS, or programming languages, because these are offered in faculty computer labs with appropriate specialist assistance.

Print Resources

The KC forms part of the main university library, so it is well integrated into students' library experiences. Its mission is to be a one-stop shop where students can complete assignments, put together group projects, or obtain help with assignments. Printed materials from the rest of the library circulate in the KC; the KC itself offers a core collection of reference books, software manuals, and study guides.

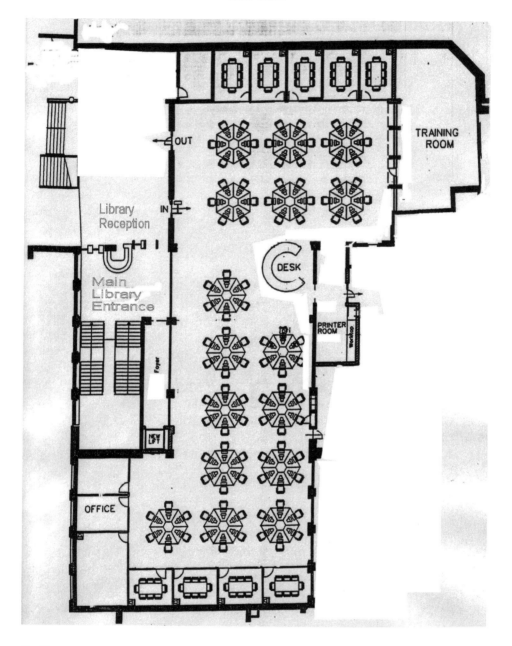

Staff

A new KC unit was created from existing posts. The manager of the KC is also responsible for managing and coordinating training in UCT libraries. Her KC unit consists of 1.5 professional librarians and two paraprofessionals. Most importantly, the KC employs thirty "student navigators" who are intensively trained in both people skills and ICT. They speak several of South Africa's eleven official languages and are a major contributor to the success of the KC. These student workers are recruited in the same systematic way as permanent staff, and are paid top rates among the student workers employed in the rest of UCT Libraries.

KC staff and navigators are particularly customer focused; they constantly rove the floor and cope proactively with frequently hectic demand. Apart from IT specialists on the library's staff, student navigators are the most competent in ICT applications. They work closely with UCT's Centre for Educational Technology, which is responsible for developing skills in course management software. The more complex technical support comes from the library IT staff.

Funding/Budget

Donors initially covered part of the capital works and the PCs; however, all recurrent funding is entirely from the UCT libraries' budget.

The KC is equipped with new PCs at the start of each academic year; the year-old PCs are rolled out to information desks and user areas in the rest of the libraries on a cascading program.

Publicity/Promotion

Apart from the libraries' website, the KC does not need to publicize itself. Queues are the norm, so it is almost a victim of its own success. It is on the orientation route for new students at the start of every academic year, and it is a constant showpiece on the university's Open Days and for important donors.

Evaluation

UCT libraries are currently administering the LibQUAL+ survey. The door count is measured by a turnstile at the door. Hourly statistics are kept of users at the PCs, in group study rooms, and in the queue.

◆

UNIVERSITY OF CINCINNATI
LANGSAM LIBRARY
CINCINNATI, OHIO, USA

Total student enrollment: 33,085
Carnegie classification: Doctoral research institution
Date established: 2002
Name: Info Commons at Langsam Library (Info Commons)
Square footage of the information commons area: 46,840 square feet
Square footage of the building: 206,209 square feet
Location: Main library
Typical access hours per week: 101
Typical service hours per week: 101
Number of service points: 4
Number of computers available for use: 76 in the Info Commons, 10 in the Student Technology Resource Center, 78 in the Computer Labs, 39 in the Classrooms

Average monthly door count: 70,785
Average monthly service transactions: 2,293
Workstation sessions/logins: Not available
Relevant URLs:
Information Commons website: www.libraries.uc.edu/services/reference/
  infocommons/

Purpose

  The Info Commons was developed as a first-stop service point in Langsam
Library to create a friendly and inviting environment where all questions are welcome. The library moved from a two-desk model of reference staffing—an information desk with graduate students and a reference consultation desk staffed by
librarians—to student peer mentors and librarians working side-by-side to serve
library users. The new service model provides an appropriate mix of approach-
able, enthusiastic, and user-friendly people to work with students. This model
was also the library's response to a campus-wide effort that addressed improvement in retention and serving undergraduates.

  The Student Technology Resource Center (STRC) was developed to meet a
growing demand for technological support. The STRC was designed as a self-
production facility for course-related multimedia projects, with library staff and
student peer mentors available to assist with applications. Adjacent to the STRC,
Multimedia Services provides multimedia equipment, including laptop computers, data projectors, digital cameras, and camcorders, for checkout by students,

staff, and faculty members. The primary focus of service to users is to provide personalized assistance with their library and research needs, as well as trouble-shooting of hardware, software, and printing.

Services

The Info Commons, STRC, and computerized instructional classrooms are services provided through university libraries. The Info Commons, launched in January 2002, is one of four service points on the main floor of Langsam Library. It is dedicated to helping users with their library and research needs and to assisting them in acquiring effective information-seeking skills. Located within the Multimedia Services department, the STRC is designed to help students with instructional technology needs, and was rolled out in fall 2002. The STRC offers multimedia equipment and a suite of multimedia software for completing class assignments and projects. Two computerized classrooms are available for library instruction sessions.

Additional services are offered in the main library in collaboration with other units on campus. Three computer labs—two PC and one Mac—are managed by the campus IT department. The Mac lab was added in winter 2003. The Center for the Enhancement of Teaching and Learning office and classroom offers resources and services for assisting faculty members in their teaching endeavors, and was opened in December 2004 in partnership with the Provost's Office.

Software

Info Commons workstations offer web access, a wealth of library and information resources, chat reference application, campus e-mail client, and Blackboard courseware. Microsoft Office software applications and various web plug-ins have been added recently. Network printing is available for all workstations.

The workstations in the STRC offer the technology and software for students to design web pages using Dreamweaver, Frontpage, and HTML; convert one file format to another; create CDs; scan images and work with Photoshop, Photo Editor, and Microsoft imaging; create presentations in PowerPoint, Flash, and Lectora; work with nonlinear digital editing technology; and create MPEGs. Library IT co-op students and staff assist with all applications.

Print Resources

Ready reference titles and oversized atlases are located next to the Info Commons desk for easy access. Other collections in close proximity include reference, government documents, videos, new-books shelf, and an enrichment reading collection of current books.

Staff

Student peer mentors staff the Info Commons all hours that the library is open. The peer mentors are mostly undergraduate students—many recruited from the honors program—trained to offer personalized assistance in navigating the

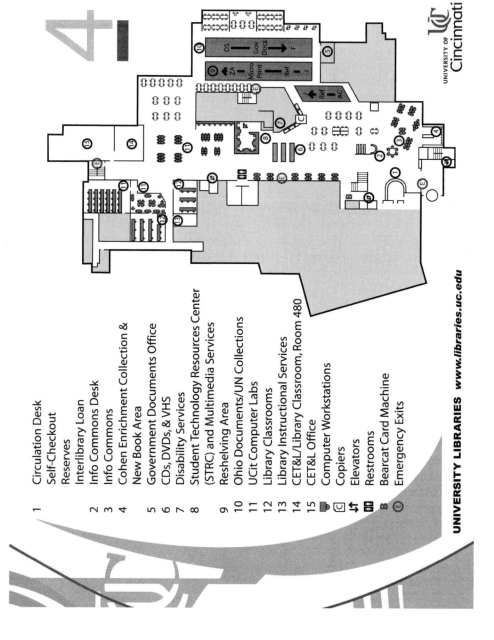

4

1   Circulation Desk
     Self-Checkout
     Reserves
     Interlibrary Loan
2   Info Commons Desk
3   Info Commons
4   Cohen Enrichment Collection &
     New Book Area
5   Government Documents Office
6   CDs, DVDs, & VHS
7   Disability Services
8   Student Technology Resources Center
     (STRC) and Multimedia Services
9   Reshelving Area
10   Ohio Documents/UN Collections
11   UCit Computer Labs
12   Library Classrooms
13   Library Instructional Services
14   CET&L/Library Classroom, Room 480
15   CET&L Office
     Computer Workstations
     Copiers
     Elevators
     Restrooms
B   Bearcat Card Machine
E   Emergency Exits

UNIVERSITY OF Cincinnati

UNIVERSITY LIBRARIES *www.libraries.uc.edu*

libraries' website, introducing the online catalog, selecting and searching basic databases to find articles, locating books in the stacks, and referring to a librarian or subject specialist as necessary. An extensive training program includes a two-day workshop prior to the fall term, weekly written assignments, two seminar sessions per quarter, and customer-service training.

A librarian serves as coordinator of the Info Commons, and a full-time support staff member serves as the evening and weekend student supervisor. Librarians and staff from the Reference and Instructional Services department also work in the Info Commons 70 percent of the library's open hours. Several of the librarians are subject specialists in the humanities, social sciences, and business.

Funding/Budget

Multiple sources of funds support the Info Commons, including general funds, student technology fees, and designated state funds for technology and retention. Computers and network printers are on a four-year replacement cycle.

Publicity/Promotion

Marketing and public awareness programs include articles featured in university and library publications, on-campus presentations and workshops, promotional materials and signs, and general promotion of services during library instruction and summer orientation sessions.

Evaluation

An annual survey is conducted during spring quarter to gather information about user traits, library and research needs, and overall satisfaction with the service provided by student peer mentors and librarians. Survey results for 2005 indicate that 85 percent of the students who use the Info Commons are undergraduates (the primary target group). Users have a wide range of information and research needs, feel comfortable asking for help with course-related assignments, and overall, are pleased with the service provided.

◆

THE UNIVERSITY OF IOWA
HARDIN LIBRARY FOR THE HEALTH SCIENCES
IOWA CITY, IOWA, USA

Total student enrollment: 28,000
Carnegie classification: Doctoral research institution
Date established: 1996; doubled in size in 1999
Name: Information Commons (Commons)
Square footage of the information commons area: 10,000 square feet
Square footage of the building: Not available

Location: The Information Commons is a distinct facility that occupies most of the second floor of the Hardin Library for the Health Sciences; building entrances are on third (primary) and first (secondary) floors.

Typical access hours per week: 96
Typical service hours per week: 96
Number of service points: 2
Number of computers available for use: 104
Average monthly door count: Not available
Average monthly service transactions: Not available
Workstation sessions/logins: Not available
Relevant URLs:
Information Commons website: www.lib.uiowa.edu/commons/
Information Commons Production Services: www.lib.uiowa.edu/commons/icps/

Purpose

When approached in 1995 by College of Medicine administrators about the possibility of securing space for an electronic classroom in the Hardin Library for the Health Sciences, library administrators countered with a proposal to create a more expansive facility, similar to the main library's Information Arcade (1992). Based on that earlier facility's successful model of collaborative planning, the Information Commons became a broader health sciences campus initiative and involved faculty stakeholders from various health colleges, IT specialists, and librarians. Many of the lessons learned by the Information Arcade planning and design initiative were applied to the Information Commons. The Hardin Library "InfoLab," as it was first termed, was designed to include a comfortable, fifty-seat hands-on electronic classroom, individual and group workstation carrels beyond the classroom, a small cluster of multimedia development workstations, and a staffed service desk.

The Information Commons opened its doors in August 1996. Two years later, in response to overwhelming user demand, construction began on an expansion that doubled the size of the facility. Opened in August 1999, the new area featured a second electronic classroom designed for workstation flexibility and learner-centered instructional sessions, a wired/wireless small-group study room, and more individual/group workstation carrels.

The goal of the Commons is to serve as the premier central delivery venue for health sciences multimedia courseware, innovative classroom instruction, health-related research, and independent learning. The Commons is guided by a tripartite mission of improving teaching, increasing access to educational resources, and exploring new technologies.

Services

At its launch in 1996, the Information Commons provided technology assistance and consultation, as well as access to educational multimedia CD-ROM titles, office productivity software, e-mail and campus networks, Internet/web resources, and multimedia authoring hardware/software. The Commons was established as a separate physical presence within Hardin Library, with its own service desk, but with an understanding that complex reference questions would be referred appropriately to the information/reference desk on a different floor.

The Commons continues to offer walk-up technical support at the service desk for individual patrons using Commons multimedia workstations, open-access stations, or electronic classroom resources. One-on-one or small-group consultation is also provided for advanced issues related to digital media production, web, electronic publishing, and information design.

By partnering with individuals and departments, the Commons extends the traditional service role of the library into more entrepreneurial ventures in multimedia authoring, digitization, publishing, information design, and application development. In 1998, the Commons established a revenue-generating Production Services unit that creates content, databases, websites, multimedia titles, and more (see link listed above). Production Services further empowers client self-sufficiency through its follow-up user consultations, thus helping clients to maintain technology products and/or projects themselves.

The Commons also handles electronic classroom scheduling and support. A variety of workshops and seminars on web and multimedia development topics were conducted between 1996 and 2000, but this type of formal, scheduled classroom instruction was discontinued based on an assessment of impact and health science campus needs.

Software

From its inception, the Commons has provided access to the networked electronic resources and databases of the UI library system as well as software for word processing, citation management, computer-based learning titles, website authoring, office productivity, and e-mail. Four multimedia stations are equipped with scanning, video/audio editing software, and a host of associated tools. These multimedia stations allow users to capture and edit video and audio and to perform OCR (optical character recognition) and slide scanning. These stations sport DV decks, cassette decks, and other audio input devices, and flatbed and slide scanners. All Commons software is supported by graduate and undergraduate student assistants. The Commons also provides access to the major software applications available campus-wide (office applications, statistical packages, website

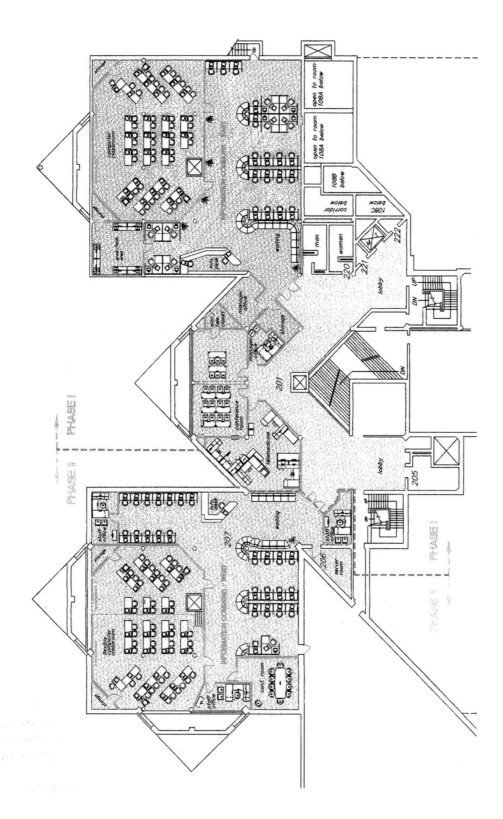

creation, CD and DVD burning, and image manipulation software). Wireless networking is also supported here.

Print Resources

The Commons provides a small monographic reference collection focused on software use and design principles. Its serials collection ranges from computing journals to topics of technology in pedagogy. The Commons circulates multimedia CD-ROMs on health sciences subjects. Prior to 2002, the Commons was primarily an "all-digital" facility, but in 2002 all nonprint media became centralized in the Commons. These resources include microfilm/fiche as well as a small collection of analog videotapes (VHS and older).

Staff

The Commons desks are staffed by student assistants when the building is open. During "workday" hours (8 a.m. to 5 p.m.), three full-time staff members (IT specialists and librarians) are also available for more complex support questions.

Production Services units consist of three half-time graduate assistants, one or two student assistants (depending on the project), a full-time digital media projects manager (instructional developer), and one full-time librarian who provides administrative strategic guidance. The service also relies on associated production assistance from one library assistant (web developer).

Funding/Budget

Campus Services (central IT services) refreshes workstations on approximately a three-year cycle, and base software licenses are drawn from a university-wide pool. The Commons acquisitions budget of $25,000 covers additional specialized software as well as multimedia CD-ROMs and research datasets on CD-ROM. Computer peripherals and electronic classroom AV equipment items are funded from income generated by Production Services. The library's general budget funds all Commons personnel, with the exception of an occasional grant-funded graduate assistant.

Publicity/Promotion

Commons professional staff members are actively involved in campus-wide IT initiatives, instructional technology committees within the health colleges, and outreach through consultations. The Commons publicizes its activities and resources through a regular e-mail newsletter, an online blog, and public relations and news releases.

The Commons is included in all tours of the Hardin Library and is featured in welcome packets for new faculty in the health colleges. Awareness of the Commons is generated by word-of-mouth among faculty and students, and by librarians in outreach and instructional sessions. Many students also gain exposure to the Commons when they attend class sessions hosted in the Commons classrooms.

Evaluation

The Commons has not conducted any evaluations. A formal self-study is planned for late 2005.

◆

University of Iowa
Information Arcade
Iowa City, Iowa, USA

Total student enrollment: 28,000
Carnegie classification: Doctoral research institution
Date established: 1992
Name: Information Arcade (formal); Arcade (colloquial)
Square footage of the information commons area: 5,700 square feet
Square footage of the building: 425,000 square feet
Location: Main library, northwest corner of first floor near building entrance
Typical access hours per week: 71.5
Typical service hours per week: 71.5
Number of service points: 1
Number of computers available for use: 56 (81 including both computers at dual-platform stations)
Average monthly door count: 5,200
Average monthly service transactions: 2,400
Workstation sessions/logins: Not available
Relevant URLs:
Information Arcade website: www.lib.uiowa.edu/arcade/

Purpose

In 1989, University of Iowa faculty members, librarians, and academic computing staff formed a group to discuss building a new state-of-the-art classroom. The "Research and Writing Electronic Center," as it was originally described, was envisioned as an electronic classroom and a cluster of workstations in the University of Iowa's main library, focused on using technology to encourage new approaches to research and writing. The Information Arcade opened its doors in September 1992.

The specific stated goals of the Arcade were: 1) student literacy within the expanding context of electronic information, with particular emphasis on analytical and written skills; 2) scholarly creativity through the use of new technologies and information resources for teaching and research; and 3) integration of innovative information technologies throughout the university curriculum.

Services

At its launch, the Arcade addressed its goals by providing assistance and consultation from librarians, graduate students, and technologists, as well as access

to traditional library holdings and CD-ROM databases, word processors and citation managers, electronic mail and computer networks, and state-of-the-art computing stations and peripherals. The Arcade was established as a separate physical presence in the main library with its own help desk, with the understanding that complex reference questions would be forwarded to the nearby reference desk.

Arcade staff currently provide information and reference service to individual patrons at the Arcade's multimedia workstations. This includes application support and troubleshooting, as well as advice in areas such as video creation, web design, and image and text manipulation. The Arcade also offers user education and consultation services, and schedules and supports the electronic classroom. Arcade staff members provide course-related instruction on web and multimedia development, as well as a variety of other workshops and seminars. One-on-one or small-group consultation is also available to address advanced issues associated with the scholarly use of multimedia and the web. Users can make appointments with any consultant; these consultations usually last from one to five hours.

The Arcade also assists with short-term and long-term research and development projects. Projects may be pilot projects or ongoing initiatives that support the Information Arcade's mission. In these projects, a consultant is assigned to work with a group of faculty, library staff, or other university personnel on a sophisticated or innovative use of technology in an academic setting.

Software

Initially, the Arcade provided access to the library's CD-ROM databases, as well as word processing, citation management, and electronic mail software. Two multimedia stations were equipped with scanning software and a scanner, and with QuickTime and a VCR.

Today, several high-end multimedia stations allow users to capture and edit video and audio and to perform OCR and slide scanning. These stations sport DV decks, cassette decks, and other audio input devices, and flatbed and slide scanners. All Arcade software is supported by graduate and student assistants, although at peak times patrons are referred to the campus help desk for aid with basic office applications. The Arcade also provides access to the major software applications that are available campus-wide (office applications, statistical packages, website creation, CD and DVD burning, and image manipulation software).

Print Resources

The Arcade provides a small monographic reference collection that is focused on software use and design principles. The Arcade's serials collection ranges from computing journals to topics of technology in pedagogy. The Arcade also circulates multimedia CD-ROMs on subjects from literature to history to religion, selected and purchased by Arcade staff and subject bibliographers.

Staff

The Arcade desk is staffed at all open hours with one graduate assistant and one student assistant, or one graduate assistant and the library assistant. Graduate assistants and student assistants come from a variety of backgrounds; this diversity is encouraged.

The Arcade staff is comprised of six graduate assistants (also called Arcade consultants), a small, variable number of student assistants, 1.0 FTE library assistant, and 1.0 FTE librarian. The Arcade also relies for technical assistance on one liaison from the library's IT staff. Arcade staff provide all patron desk help and project consultation. While Arcade staff provide first-tier technology troubleshooting, difficult or persistent workstation problems are referred to the IT liaison. Campus Services (a subunit of Campus IT) provides further help and deals with any printer networking problems. Campus IT provides the base workstation image with common software, which the liaison and select Arcade staff modify before deploying in the Arcade.

Funding/Budget

Campus Services refreshes workstations on roughly a three-year basis, and base software licenses are drawn from a university-wide pool. The Arcade acquisitions budget of $30,000 covers additional software as well as monographs, serials, and CD-ROMs. Computer peripherals are funded from the library's general budget

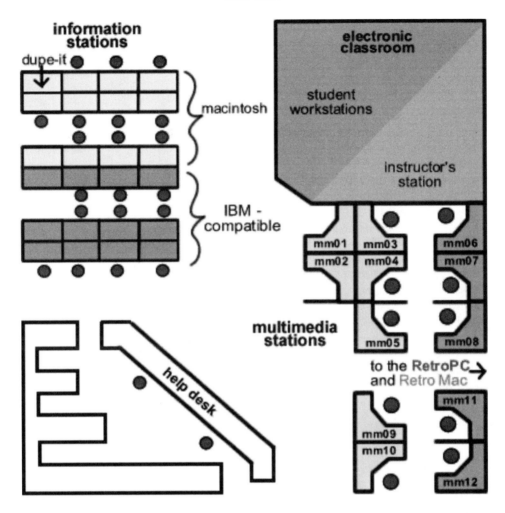

and are not granted a set yearly amount. The library's budget also funds all Arcade personnel.

Publicity/Promotion

The Arcade is included in all tours of the main library and is mentioned briefly in the libraries section of new faculty and staff orientation. Awareness of the Arcade is generated by word-of-mouth among faculty and students. In addition, many students gain exposure to the Arcade when they attend classes in the Arcade classroom.

Evaluation

The Arcade has a web survey available on its homepage, but the best gauge of user satisfaction has come from direct user feedback and observable traffic patterns.

In 2003, the Arcade surveyed small focus groups to gain more formal input on user satisfaction.

University of Minnesota–Twin Cities
Wilson Library
Minneapolis, Minnesota, USA

Total student enrollment: 45,413
Carnegie classification: Doctoral research institution
Date established: 2004
Name: Information Commons
Square footage of the information commons area: 775 square feet
Square footage of the building: 248,000 square feet
Location: Wilson Library
Typical access hours per week: 100
Typical service hours per week: 87
Number of service points: 1
Number of computers available for use: 35
Average monthly door count: 8,000
Average monthly service transactions: 750
Workstation sessions/logins: Not available
Relevant URLs:
Information Commons website: www.lib.umn.edu/about/undergrad/infocommons/

Purpose

In 2002, the University of Minnesota Libraries created an Undergraduate Initiatives Council charged with supporting and enhancing the undergraduate library experience. As an initial step, the council conducted a series of focus groups and interviews designed to help the libraries better understand undergraduate students, and to identify and prioritize potential initiatives that would make an impact on them. A follow-up survey revealed that 81 percent wanted "one place where students can research and write their papers with librarians, writing tutors, and computer assistants all there."

The University Libraries placed a request in a University Compact Proposal for monetary support for this initiative and soon thereafter received adequate funding to construct and run a modest-sized information commons.

Services

The Information Commons contains a help desk where patrons can ask technology reference, research reference, and directional questions. The help desk did not replace the reference desk, so there are not many research reference questions—

patrons tend to go to the main reference desk for these services. Answering technology reference questions is a new service offered by the libraries.

Software

Thirty-one productivity PCs offer Microsoft Office 2003, Adobe Photoshop Elements, and Adobe GoLive. Two productivity Macs include Microsoft Office 2003, Adobe Photoshop Elements, Adobe GoLive, iPhoto, iMovie, and iDVD. One multimedia PC and one multimedia Mac offer a combination of Microsoft Office 2003, Adobe Creative Suite (Acrobat, Illustrator, Image Ready, InDesign, Photoshop), Macromedia Studio (Dreamweaver, Fireworks, Flash, Freehand), Adobe Premiere Pro, scanning software (including OCR), and Final Cut Studio (DVD Studio Pro, Final Cut Pro, Motion 2, Soundtrack Pro). The Information Commons staff provides one-on-one support for all software available in the IC. The paraprofessional and one of the librarians are the primary technology experts.

Print Resources

The Information Commons (IC) owns and lends in-house user manuals for all software on IC computers. In addition, the IC is in one of the main libraries, so it is located among a rich supply of print resources. Many patrons use the IC to

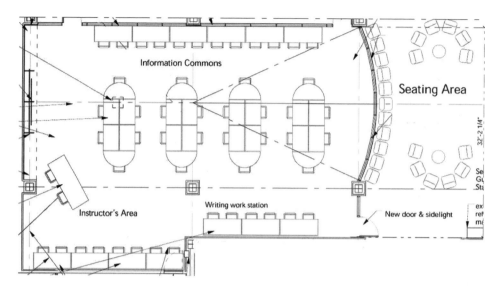

scan materials from the collections, and some librarians use the print reference collection to assist patrons.

Staff

The IC is staffed by a combination of eleven librarians, one paraprofessional, and four student workers. One librarian and the paraprofessional were hired with service in the IC specifically outlined in their position descriptions. The remaining ten librarians are from the reference, collection development, and Undergraduate Initiatives departments. These librarians each staff the IC for one to three hours per week.

The librarians have varying degrees of technical expertise. Training for librarians focuses mostly on Microsoft Office (Word, Excel, PowerPoint) and scanning software.The paraprofessional was hired primarily for his technical expertise. He is the resident expert on video editing, graphic design, and web design, although several librarians also have skills in these areas. The paraprofessional is also a liaison between IC staff and the library IT department, which oversees the hardware for the IC.

Student workers are recruited primarily through previous work in the University Libraries. They are trained on both research reference and technology skills.

Funding/Budget

The University Libraries received $180,000 in one-time funds and $69,000 in recurring funds for the facility. A task force made up of members from the Facilities, IT, Reference, Circulation, and Undergraduate Initiatives departments worked with an external architect to plan and construct the facility. The budget for the facility is administered through the director of the Humanities and Social Science department, who is the head of reference and instruction services for the Wilson Library, where the Information Commons is located.

Publicity/Promotion

The IC has been covered in a campus newspaper article and has placed ads in the student newspaper. A website and flyers are also used to promote the facility. During the summer of 2005, IC staff plan to create a brochure to advertise the facility to faculty members.

Evaluation

IC staff keep consistent statistics on seat count and questions asked in the Information Commons. In addition, in February 2005, two surveys were administered (one as a pop-up in a web browser with one question: "How satisfied were you with the IC today?" the other as a paper survey). The library plans to continue to administer surveys and hold focus group sessions in order to determine what students need from the IC.

◄◆►

UNIVERSITY OF NEVADA–LAS VEGAS
LIED LIBRARY
LAS VEGAS, NEVADA, USA

Total student enrollment: 20,076
Carnegie classification: Doctoral research institution
Date established: 2001
Name: Lied Library
Square footage of the information commons area: 300,000 square feet
Square footage of the building: 300,000 square feet
Location: Main library
Typical access hours per week: 100
Typical service hours per week: 100
Number of service points: 2
Number of computers available for use: 220
Average monthly door count: 121,000
Average monthly service transactions: 3,800 (computer help desk)
Workstation sessions/logins: Not available
Relevant URLs: Not available

Purpose

The creation of the Information Commons stemmed from a desire to make the library the hub for scholarly endeavors on campus and to create a space that simultaneously supported the acquisition of knowledge, collaborative work, and completion of a final product. The goal was a more convenient and efficient

method of providing service to patrons, allowing them help with both information and technology questions within easy reach of one another.

Services

The research and information desk was merged with the computer help desk to provide more centralized services. Some functions of the computer help desk, such as personal laptop authentication, library laptop checkout, and the multimedia design studio, were previously handled by campus computing services. The Information Commons was merged with Media Resources to form a new Media and Computer Services department. This department provides support for all computing activities, as well as media viewing and collection development.

Software

All the computers have access to a 100 mbps network and Novell client login, and have a Windows policy restrictions for security and limitations. Available at most workstations are Microsoft Office 2003, Photoshop Elements, Macromedia Dreamweaver, Firefox, Internet Explorer, Telnet, and FTP. Specialized software at media/multimedia workstations are all of the above, plus Pinnacle, Ulead, Adobe Acrobat, Adobe Photoshop, Adobe Illustrator, Macromedia Flash, and Macromedia Fireworks.

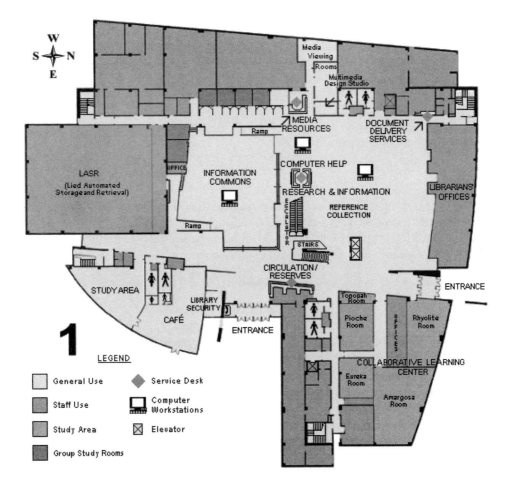

Print Resources

Computers are located on all five floors of the library, in close proximity to the circulating, reference, and microforms collections. Media items can be viewed on a selected number of PCs and clips can be captured for use. Computer-based microforms scanners allow capture to JPEG or PDF formats, which can be printed or saved to disk.

Staff

Media and Computer Services has a full-time staff of seven (one librarian and six classified staff members) and twelve to fifteen student employees per semester. Students stationed at the computer help desk rove across all five floors to monitor printers and provide computer assistance. The support desk is covered by at least one person all hours the library is open. During peak times, there may be two or more people on duty at any given time.

Funding/Budget

Replacement public workstations, new software, and other equipment are paid for through the student technology fee, which is collected and disbursed through campus IT services. Staffing is funded through the library's budget.

Publicity/ Promotion

No information has been provided.

Evaluation

The primary method for evaluating services has been through surveys. The library participates in LibQual, which includes questions on satisfaction with technology. The library also administers a paper survey each semester to evaluate patron satisfaction with library laptop checkout.

◆

UNIVERSITY OF NEWCASTLE
AUCHMUTY LIBRARY
NEWCASTLE, NEW SOUTH WALES, AUSTRALIA

Total student enrollment: 25,000
Carnegie classification: Doctoral research institution
Date established: 2003
Name: Auchmuty Information Common (formal); AIC or Infocommon (colloquial)
Square footage of the information commons area: 6,620 square feet
Square footage of the building: 120,654 square feet
Location: Main library, level two
Typical access hours per week: 136
Typical service hours per week: 136
Number of service points: 1
Number of computers available for use: 112
Average monthly door count: 34,596 (average for first semester 2005)
Average monthly service transactions: 3,400
Workstation sessions/logins: Not available
Relevant URLs:
Auchmuty Information Common website: www.newcastle.edu.au / service / library / aic / index.html

Purpose

The Information Common was established to enrich patrons' learning and research experience by implementing collaborative and individual workstations in an informal atmosphere where staff assistance and support are available on a twenty-four-hour basis during the week. A café service is available during business hours; lounge areas create a welcoming environment. The AIC promotes the

library's extensive online resources with staff expertise to assist with information discovery and evaluation, and supports the library's evolution to a hybrid library service that provides access to online and print resources and associated services.

Services

The information desk in the AIC provides a wide range of services. Patrons receive assistance with research and information discovery, including print and online resources, IT support, general information, and software sales. Laptops are also available for loan. The area provides wireless connectivity. The reference service was previously located on level three of the library and software sales had its own shop front. The new information desk saw the combination of reference, IT, and software sales in one location. Complex reference queries are referred to the faculty librarians. The rover service (students who provide proactive IT support) was a new service created for the AIC environment. A training laboratory for information literacy programs is available with seating for fifteen participants.

Software

All machines in the AIC have a comprehensive set of software. The software image includes a web browser, campus e-mail client, library applications, Microsoft

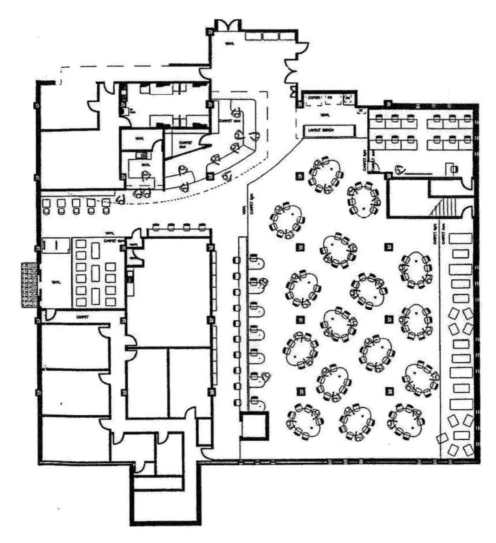

Office suite, and statistical packages. Users can also access the student administration and tutorial registration system. Assistance is provided for all software packages installed in the AIC. The image is updated every semester to ensure software is the latest version.

Print Resources

The AIC is located on level two of the Auchmuty Library on the Callaghan campus. A ready reference collection, newspaper, and new-book displays are available in the AIC. The library's print and nonbook collections are available on levels one, three, and four. Access to all services, including the AIC, is available between 8 a.m. and 10 p.m. on weekdays, and 9 a.m. to 5 p.m. on weekends. When the AIC operates on weeknights between 10 p.m. and 8 a.m., the print collections are not available.

Staff

Patron needs are met by staff with a range of skills. During the day, three staff members are assigned to the area: a reference librarian, an IT specialist, and a rover. The group provides research and reference advice, IT support, and general information. The role of the rover is to provide first-line support to users with IT and general questions, including software support, printer maintenance, and software sales.

Funding/Budget

The library received funding from a strategic initiative fund to implement the Information Common, supplemented by funds from the library's operations budget. Staffing is funded from the library's operations budget. An architect and trades services were coordinated by the university's Facilities Management Office. The café is operated by a nonuniversity vendor.

Publicity/Promotion

The Information Common is promoted in the library's orientation tours, including the virtual library tour of the Auchmuty Library. Each year, information about the AIC and postcards advertising its services are sent to student residence halls. As part of the library, the AIC was also included in the University Orientation Week program and advertised in the Student Union diary in 2005.

Evaluation

Quantitative data indicates that the Information Common is students' preferred place of study, with a 20 percent increase in the gate count in 2004 compared with 2003. The Information Common operates at 80 to 100 percent capacity between 8 a.m. and 10 p.m., and 50 to 60 percent between 10 p.m. and 8 a.m. Feedback from users is extremely positive. A survey of use of the facility, services offered, and client behavior will be undertaken in second semester 2005. The use of online resources has also increased since the AIC was opened.

◀━━

UNIVERSITY OF NORTH CAROLINA AT CHAPEL HILL
WALTER ROYAL DAVIS LIBRARY
CHAPEL HILL, NORTH CAROLINA, USA

Total student enrollment: 23,913
Carnegie classification: Doctoral research institution
Date established: 1994
Name: Information Commons (formal), Info Commons (colloquial)
Square footage of the information commons area: 5,704 square feet
Square footage of the building: 422,659 square feet
Location: Main library, entrance floor

Typical access hours per week: 103
Typical service hours per week: 84
Number of service points: 1
Number of computers available for use: 118
Average monthly door count: 89,700
Average monthly service transactions: 3,652
Workstation sessions/logins: Not available
Relevant URLs: Not available

Purpose

The Information Commons was established in 1997. Prior to the implementation of the Information Commons, an Electronic Information Service (EIS) that opened in 1994 provided the library's first four public Windows workstations for Internet access, as well as access to specialized CD-ROMs and a scanner. The EIS area was staffed by reference staff at a separate desk. This area expanded rapidly.

In 1997, the library replaced existing limited function catalog terminals with thirty Windows-based Internet stations located in an area on the first floor that had been occupied by the card catalog. The EIS machines, more in number by now, moved over to the reconfigured reference area. The service desk help-staff in both areas, and reference staff began roving the area to help patrons.

The library has added more terminals each year; there are currently 118 Info Commons computers. There are four public scanners, three CD-ROM stations with preinstalled applications, and three stations where patrons can install their own CDs or those from the library's collection that are not preinstalled. There are also four GIS stations and four stations for government documents, applications, and data. There are printers for e-docs and a plotter for GIS applications, as well as fee-based laser printing available from each Info Commons workstation.

Services

EIS continues to facilitate scanning, textual analysis, OCR, and statistical analysis, as well as access to specialized Internet databases, GIS information, CD-ROM materials, Internet multimedia files, and government resources. EIS supports these applications in a specific area of the Info Commons close to the reference desk. Other areas of the IC that do not include scanners, multimedia capability, or CD-ROMs are also supported by EIS and reference staff. All Information Commons areas have access to wireless networking, and wireless laptops are available at a nearby circulation desk.

Software

All Info Commons workstations are configured with a standard suite of software that includes Internet Explorer, Mozilla, the Microsoft Office Suite (Word, Access, Excel, Publisher, Powerpoint, Image Editor/Viewers), IrfanView, Paint, RealPlayer, QuickTime, Windows Media Player, HostEx, SSH Secure Shell, WS FTP, AFS, InterVideo WinDVD player, Create CD, CAJ Viewer, DVI Viewer, GSview 4.6, Alternatiff, Narrator, Magnifier, Notepad, and Wordpad. Some workstations include login software that restricts access to only faculty, staff, and students. This allows enhanced access to university resources made available via central IT service units and the library.

Print Resources

The Information Commons is located on the first floor in close proximity to the large reference print collection. The reference section of the Info Commons is directly adjacent to several of the ready reference rows (biography, book reviews, and major literary criticism series); just beyond lies the rest of the print collection. The reference desk holds a ready reference collection as well, accessible to patrons when they need it.

Staff

The Info Commons help desk is the main reference desk; it offers long service hours that include nights and weekends. The desk is staffed by fourteen professional librarians, six reference paraprofessionals, and nine graduate students. Most of the graduate students are seeking MLS degrees, although there are

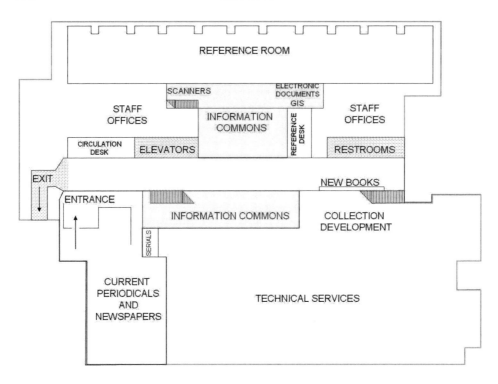

occasionally students from other disciplines. Typically three to four people staff the desk during the fall and spring semesters, and two or three during the summer. All but one of the librarians work in the Reference department as their home department; one works in Systems.

There are typically about five hours of general and specialized reference subject training for new staff. Newer desk staff are initially paired with more experienced staff. During the fall and spring semesters, one person during each shift is a designated rover in the Info Commons.

Software and hardware support for Info Commons computers is provided primarily by specially trained Library Systems staff located in the reference department, in conjunction with network engineers and support specialists who manage the overall library IT infrastructure.

Funding/Budget

There is currently no budget specifically for the Info Commons. The provost authorized one-time funding for workstations in 1997, but for the next six years Info Commons equipment needs competed with all other library IT needs. In 2004, the library began to receive machines recycled from computer labs around campus, some of which had a year of warranty hardware service still in effect. In recent months, a small group of library staff began to meet to discuss low- or no-cost ways of improving the Info Commons and to create a planning document for library administration that includes options for redesigning the IC and associated costs.

The more specialized workstations (scanning, GIS, CD-ROM) have generally been replaced on a three-year life cycle. These computers were funded as part of the annual IT budget planning process.

Publicity/Promotion

The Info Commons is featured on library orientation tours conducted throughout the year and has been highlighted in past issues of the annual newspaper that welcomes students, faculty, and staff to campus. There is no formal publicity program focused on the Info Commons; students are primarily aware of the facility and its service offerings through word-of-mouth advertising. Library staff are considering ways to highlight the Info Commons on the library website.

Evaluation

The Library Systems department has conducted staff feedback sessions to solicit suggestions for improving the software and features of Info Commons workstations; it maintains a website for comments and suggestions. Additional feedback sessions are planned for students and faculty, and suggestions calling for extensive change will be included in future planning documents.

◄►

UNIVERSITY OF WATERLOO
WILLIAM G. DAVIS CENTRE LIBRARY
WATERLOO, ONTARIO, CANADA

Total student enrollment: 22,800
Carnegie classification: Doctoral research institution
Date established: 2004
Name: RBC Information Commons; InfoCommons
Square footage of the information commons area: 1,132 square feet
Square footage of the building: 50,023 square feet
Location: One space, shared with other campus organizations
Typical access hours per week: 106 (first 12 weeks of term); 162 (last 4 weeks)
Typical service hours per week: 56
Number of service points: 1
Number of computers available for use: 39 in the Info Commons; 37, Express (standing)
Average monthly door count: 85,017
Average monthly service transactions: Not available
Workstation sessions/logins: Not available
Relevant URLs:
Davis Centre Library website: www.lib.uwaterloo.ca/tour/DC/quickDC.html
Davis Centre Library tour: www.lib.uwaterloo.ca/tour/DC/

Purpose

The Davis Centre Library is located on the main and lower levels of the William G. Davis Computer Research Centre. It houses materials in the fields of engineering, mathematics, and science. The RBC Information Commons provides a comfortable work environment containing thirty-nine full-service multimedia computer workstations with access to Microsoft Office, the Internet, and more.

Services

The newest service doubles the number of computers in the library and provides comfortable office chair seating for thirty-nine users. Computers in the InfoCommons are faster, with small-footprint flat screens, and are equipped with software that supports library research and report or project submission within the library. Another new service adjacent to the InfoCommons is eighty-four new places to plug a laptop into the Internet and a power outlet. Old study tables were retrofitted to create this group work area.

Reference and circulation services are offered from nearby service desks. Reference staff can assist with any question, including technology and Microsoft Office questions. Chat reference can also be used from the InfoCommons.

Software

Software on InfoCommons computers includes web browsers, Microsoft Office suite, RefWorks, SciFinder Scholar, and Beilstein clients.

Print Resources

The library has two floors. The InfoCommons is close to the entrance and the stairs to the lower floor collections (periodicals, government publications). The book collection on the same floor is visible from the InfoCommons. Library staff know that students use the collections because shelvers retrieve books from the InfoCommons on a regular basis.

The current resource philosophy is to provide electronic copies of periodical articles, either through license or document delivery. The library is also investing in a modest e-reference collection and e-books. The print collection will reach a finite size and will be weeded regularly for off-site storage or discard. This frees up space for services like the InfoCommons and reflects the use patterns of resources.

Staff

Reference librarians and library assistants are the main support for users of the InfoCommons. If a co-op student is added to the facility in the future, a librarian will be the supervisor and trainer. Systems department staff support the desktop image and infrastructure, as they do for all computing in the library. They also supervise co-op students who carry out some of the work. There is no coordinator position for the InfoCommons. The library has used reference staff as rovers in the past and may consider implementing this practice again in the future.

Funding/Budget

There is no staffing budget for the InfoCommons. It is part of the overall budget for reference staffing. Funding for replacement computers and software is part of the overall library IT budget.

Publicity/Promotion

The InfoCommons is visible through the floor-to-ceiling glass wall at the library entrance. There are prominent vertical signs that mark the beginning of the Info-Commons. There was campus news coverage when the facility opened; the library also handed out a pamphlet outlining what was available in the InfoCommons. Librarians describe the facility in orientation and information literacy sessions.

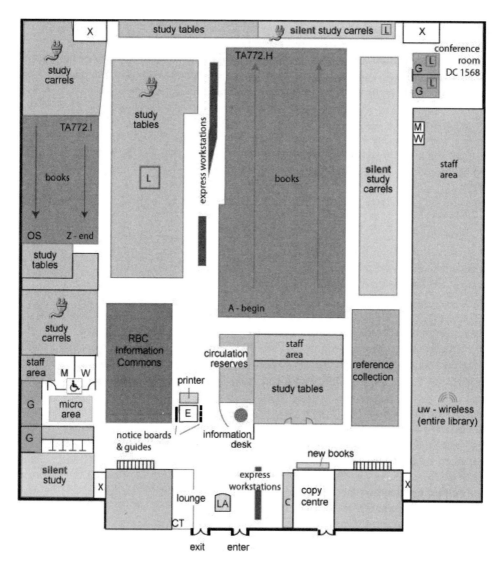

Evaluation

The InfoCommons is full by 10 a.m. most days and stays full until very late at night, particularly during exam periods. Library staff observe students working comfortably in groups at workstations, which indicates that the physical design of the desks is good. Students who use the area for the first time often tell staff how much they like it and ask the library to expand it. The library plans to do a post-occupancy evaluation in the coming year.

Afterword:
"Getting It Right"

Crit Stuart

"The academic library as the preferred destination for students is in steep decline. One imagines the physical facility soon becoming the appendix of the campus body."

This dreary forecast simulates the dismay of many academic librarians, this writer included, around ten years ago as we made note of declining attendance figures and the ascendance of the user at her desktop. Looking back at that not-so-distant time, we now know that a few of our colleagues were inspired to act rather than lament.

Until very recently, genuinely compelling, effective learning spaces were a rare commodity on campus. But now that colleges and universities have begun to support undergraduate academic success as both strategic goal and recruitment incentive, learning spaces outside the classroom have come of age. In the last few years, we have heard undergraduates reinforce the notion that the campus library is the logical host for their learning and knowledge-building efforts. And we note with some trepidation their quick-to-follow caveat that we get it right or they will gravitate elsewhere. A balance of humility for the undertaking, coupled with ingenuity and passion, are required.

Our libraries have responded by creating the student-centered enterprise that is the information commons. We face competition with other campus entities. Residential communities, tutoring services, and even academic departments are giving consideration to the amenities, technologies, and support services that will cause students to gravitate to, and dwell in, their domains. Libraries that respond with information commons, especially those that genuinely support personal reflection, communal and individual learning, communication and technology skills development, and productivity are championed by students and campus administrators. After a decade of witnessing information commons gain a foothold on campus, we have an emerging body of user opinion and data, partnership experiences, successes, and failures to inform new directions.

A handful of academic libraries have pioneered efforts to understand undergraduate productivity needs and respond with services and facilities that effectively comprehend the opportunities. The work of this vanguard is characterized by user-centered assessment and field study techniques that provide deeply informed, and frequently unexpected, insight into the academic lives of students. These libraries engage their students and faculty in sustained dialogue characterized by listening and reflection. In time, their reputation for being sensitive and inclusive significantly raises their capital across campus. The programming of undergraduate learning spaces at these libraries tends to align with the institution's educational mission, and represents a cogent response to the unique realities and culture of their campuses. These pioneering libraries successfully engage library staff and collaborators to imagine the new types of skills and training required of front-line workers, and to realign their organization to be more agile, and responsive to successive opportunities as they emerge.

In sometimes stark contrast to these informed experiments, aspiring libraries may join the information commons movement by appropriating or mimicking properties from the best installations without embracing or understanding their potential. These shortcut emulations can be big improvements over the status quo, yet may not yield the same degrees of organizational readiness and campus outreach, sensitivity for student learning needs, staff commitment, or improved models of staffing and service seen in the premiere installations. The comprehensive information commons reflects good stewardship, heartfelt attention to details and amenities, and evidence of metrics-based improvements. These commons evolve rather than remain static, and each iteration or element persists only as long as it is valued by the student consumer. We must see more libraries engage in systematic assessment and planning, reinforced by leaders who can elicit the best contributions from library staff and partners. The handful of superb information commons that have arisen through systematic discovery and well-orchestrated efforts, several of which are covered in this field guide, demonstrate the importance of understanding one's local environment and the latent possibilities to provide genuine undergraduate support. To do less is to squander the opportunity and risk losing ground to other campus entities intent on serving students.

Information commons are modeled for undergraduates, and they will continue to evolve, but there is other work to be done. Groundbreaking experimentation is being directed to facilities, resources, and services for graduate students and faculty. Libraries report increasing pressure from these "overlooked populations" to provide convening grounds for their teaching, scholarship, research, and training needs. Can we get it right for graduate students and faculty? There is every reason to think academic libraries will meet the challenge with a fresh suite of responses. A handful of libraries have completed field surveys of these populations, at times engaging anthropologists and other experts in human behavior to produce intriguing findings. Faculty and graduate students imagine the library (sometimes with other agencies) providing a rich array of helpful assets; deeper exposure to subject-specific and multidisciplinary resources; increased exposure to subject liaisons; instruction in research techniques and methodologies; guidance in communication competencies (writing, oral presentation, multimedia); exposure to schema for organizing one's personal information stores; support for writing grants and sponsored research, especially for graduate students; new forms of scholarly communication coupled with publishing assistance; new software and technology skills training; e-text and metadata consultation; socializing spaces for serendipitous or planned encounters with individuals outside one's discipline; assistance with classroom learning objects and applications that take better advantage of information resources; short-term collaboration space; and exclusive scholar's spaces and amenities for focused concentration. The world will watch intently as this first wave of libraries engineers the research commons for graduate students and faculty. We have much to learn from their efforts, even as we work to understand the opportunities at our own institutions.

Should academic libraries be in the business of delivering comprehensive dwelling, learning, productivity, and socializing spaces? In the minds of undergraduates, graduate students, and faculty who comprise the holy trinity of our campuses, the answer is overwhelmingly yes. If we build it they will come and flourish and inspire us to do the next good thing, if we can just get it right. Readers should use the examples of information commons and expert insight provided in this field guide to inspire their work. Understand that the thing you produce will mirror the passion, engagement, risk-taking, creativity, and hard work given to the effort. Our notable goal to revitalize academic libraries is just beginning.

Appendix A

◆

Field Guide Entry Survey Form

INFORMATION COMMONS FIELD GUIDE
DESCRIPTIVE ENTRY FORM AND INSTRUCTIONS FOR COMPLETION

Completing and Returning This Form
This form is to be used to enter descriptive information for an entry in the upcoming book by Scarecrow Press, *The Information Commons: A Field Guide*, hereafter simply referred to as "the field guide." Descriptive entries in the field guide characterize library integrated service programs or facilities termed either an "Information Commons," or other related terms such as "Technology Commons," "Knowledge Commons," "Learning Commons," or similar terms. If you have received this form to be filled out, you have such a program or facility that has been selected as an important candidate for inclusion in the field guide. ***All entries submitted will become the property of Scarecrow Press.*** Please read through these instructions carefully and then complete and return this form via e-mail. Please return the form as a Microsoft Word file, as we will be assembling the book manuscript from these submissions.

Photos and Other Images
All field guide entries will ideally include at least one photograph and potentially a variety of floor plans and other images of the facilities being described. We request that you include these images as either JPEG or TIFF file attachments with your form submission. Please note that any images we use will be printed in black and white. The image files should be reasonably high quality, but individual files should not be more than 1 MB in size. Please do not include files that in aggregate

will amount to more than 2 MB worth of attachments, as e-mails this large may not be transferred by many intermediary e-mail servers.

Answering the Questions

The following sections provide instructions for answering the individual questions in the entry form. If you are uncertain about how to answer a question and need guidance, please send an e-mail to the e-mail address listed above. We will get back to you with an e-mail or a phone call—whichever is most appropriate. Each of these questions provides general guidance on how to answer it, including the typical size and nature of the information sought, as well as any framing information particular to the question. The entries are divided into two parts, a quantitative section for summary data and a qualitative section for narrative response descriptions. Please fill out all of the questions to the best of your ability. In the case of some quantitative questions you may lack the specific information requested; in this situation make an informed estimate and indicate that it is an estimate.

Summary Data Questions

1. **Institution:** Please provide the name of the university or parent institution to which your library belongs, as well as the city, state/province (or territory), and country in the space below.

2. **Student Enrollment:** Please list your institution's overall student enrollment (for both undergraduate and graduate/professional degrees).

3. **Carnegie Classification:** Please check the appropriate classification for your institution:

   ❏ Doctoral research institution: During a typical year, the university awards at least ten doctoral degrees per year across three or more disciplines, or at least twenty doctoral degrees per year overall, as well as offering a wide range of baccalaureate programs.

   ❏ Master's college or university: During a typical year, the university awards at least twenty or more master's degrees.

   ❏ Baccalaureate college: A primarily undergraduate college with a major emphasis on baccalaureate programs, in which 10–50 percent of awarded degrees are baccalaureates.

   ❏ Associate's college: Offers associate's degree and certificate programs but where baccalaureate degrees account for less than 10 percent of all degrees awarded.

   ❏ Specialized institution: Offers degrees ranging from the bachelor's to the doctorate, and typically awards a majority of degrees in a single field (e.g., music or engineering).

   ❏ Tribal college or university: Tribally controlled institutions located on reservations; member of the American Indian Higher Education Consortium.

4. **Picture/Photo:** Please provide as an e-mail attachment a representative digital photograph of your information commons facility. Images should be provided as either JPEG or TIFF files, each less than 1 MB in size. *Keep in mind that images will be printed in black and white.*

5. **Floor plan or diagram:** Please provide as an e-mail attachment a representative floor plan or diagram of your information commons facility. If you do not have a floor plan, you may include typical furniture/workstation diagrams or other relevant spatial layouts. Images should be provided as either JPEG or TIFF files, each less than 1 MB in size.

6. **Year established:** Please indicate the year in which the facility or service first became available to the public.

7. **Name:** Please indicate the name most commonly used to refer to your service or facility.

8. **Square footage:**

   A. Please indicate as an integer the most accurate figure you have for the square footage of the publicly available space associated with your facility (i.e., the information commons area itself).

   B. Please also list the total square footage of the building in which the information commons is located.

9. **Location:** Please indicate which of the following options best describes the location of your facility. If you wish to elaborate with additional information, please do so. **The boxes can be checked by right-clicking on them and selecting "properties," and then "checked."**

   ❑ Main library. Details (floor, etc): _____
   ❑ Branch/special library. Details: _____
   ❑ Space shared with other campus organizations. Details: _____
   ❑ Other. Details: _____

10. **Typical access hours per week:** Please indicate as an integer the typical number of hours that the program or facility is available to its clientele during a typical academic school year week, with or without any service staff. If there are multiple service points or distinct locations, list the figure for the primary location.

11. **Typical service hours per week:** Please indicate as an integer the typical number of hours that the program or facility is available to its clientele during a

typical academic school year week, with service staff. If the facility always has service staff available, this will be the same number as the previous response. If there are multiple service points or distinct locations, list the figure for the primary location.

12. **Number of service points:** Please indicate as an integer the number of service points that you associate with this program or facility.

13. **Number of computers available for use:** Please indicate as an integer the number of computers that are available for use by the clientele of this program or facility.

14. **Average monthly door count:** Please indicate as an integer the average door count during a typical month of the academic school year.

15. **Average monthly service transactions:** Please indicate as an integer the average number of service transactions of any kind during a typical month of the academic school year, as well as any additional details of clarification.

16. **Workstation sessions/logins:** Please estimate as an integer the average number of sessions (tracked by login or otherwise recorded or estimated).

Narrative Response Questions

A. **Purpose:** Please describe the reason(s) for creating the facility in 50–200 words of narrative.

B. **Services:** Please describe the services offered in the facility in 50–200 words of narrative. Which services were new? Which ones existed prior to the establishment of the facility? Were some services a combination of new and old? Was a new service unit created? Do you still have a reference desk?

C. **Software:** Please describe the software offered in the facility in 50–200 words of narrative, including applications and utilities, as well as associated support and infrastructure.

D. **Print resources:** Please describe in 50–200 words of narrative the relationship with and proximity to print, microform, and other collections, resource integration philosophy and practice. Try to describe any ways in which the facility interacts with the print resources of your library.

E. **Staff:** Please describe in 50–200 words of narrative the staffing patterns and schedules for the facility, where positions come from, if there are rovers, and how staff are trained and recruited, what their backgrounds are, etc.

F. **Funding/Budget:** Please describe in 50–200 words of narrative the source(s) of funds, budgeting, planning, and management for the program or facility.

G. **Publicity/Promotion:** Please describe in 50–200 words of narrative any processes you have established to make the program or facility known to students, any public awareness programs, or faculty liaison publicity activities. Generally, describe any means that you undertake to make your clientele aware of the program or facility.

H. **Evaluation:** Please describe in 50–200 words any measures of success or user satisfaction that you have undertaken. How do you evaluate the program or facility?

Appendix B

◆

Time Line of Information Commons Developments

1990	Coalition for Networked Information (CNI) established
1992	University of Iowa (Iowa, United States) constructs the *Information Arcade* in the Main Library
1994	University of Southern California (California, United States) constructs the *Information Commons*
	University of North Carolina, Chapel Hill (North Carolina, United States) constructs the *Electronic Information Service*
1996	University of Iowa (Iowa, United States) constructs the *Information Commons* in the Health Sciences (Hardin) Library
1997	Lehigh University (Pennsylvania, United States) constructs the *Information Commons*
	University of North Carolina, Chapel Hill (North Carolina, United States) expands its *Electronic Information Service* area and renames this comprehensive area the *Information Commons*
1998	Emory University (Georgia, United States) constructs the *Information Commons*
	Oregon State University (Oregon, United States) constructs the *Valley Library Information Commons*
1999	Bucknell University (Pennsylvania, United States) constructs the *Information Commons*
	University of Calgary (Alberta, Canada) constructs the *Information Commons*
	University of Iowa (Iowa, United States) expands the *Information Commons* in the Health Sciences (Hardin) Library

2000   University of Cape Town (South Africa) constructs the *Knowledge Commons*

2001   Ferris State University (Michigan, United States) constructs the *Information Commons*

Kansas State University (Kansas, United States) constructs the *K-State InfoCommons*

Saint Martin's University (Washington, United States) constructs the *Information Commons*

University of Nevada, Las Vegas (Nevada, United States) constructs the *Lied Library*

2002   Georgia Institute of Technology (Georgia, United States) constructs the *Library West Commons*

Texas Christian University (Texas, United States) constructs the *Information Commons*

University of Arizona (Arizona, United States) constructs the *Information Commons*

University of Cincinnati (Ohio, United States) constructs the *Info Commons at Langsam Library*

2003   Indiana University, Bloomington (Indiana, United States) constructs the *Information Commons*

Kent State University (Ohio, United States) constructs the *Information Commons*

Simon Fraser University (British Columbia, Canada) constructs the *Information Commons*

University of Auckland (Auckland, New Zealand) constructs the *Kate Edger Information Commons*

Trinity University (Texas, United States) constructs the *Information Commons*

University of Newcastle (New South Wales, Australia) constructs the *Auchmuty Information Commons*

2004   Brigham Young University (Utah, United States) constructs the *Information Commons/General Reference*

Northwestern University (Illinois, United States) constructs the *Information Commons*

University of Auckland (Auckland, New Zealand) constructs the *Grafton Information Commons*

University of Minnesota, Twin Cities (Minnesota, United States) constructs the *Information Commons*

University of Waterloo (Ontario, Canada) constructs the *RBC Information Commons*

2005   California State Polytechnic University (California, United States) constructs the *Learning Commons* or *Digital Teaching Library*

Index

Note: Page numbers in *italics* refer to diagrams.

About the Editors
and Contributors

Janette S. Blackburn, AIA, LEED AP, is a senior associate at Shepley Bulfinch Richardson & Abbott. In her career, she has focused on the planning and design of higher education facilities that promote community and scholarship, including work with the Avery Art and Architecture, and Teachers College libraries for Columbia University, and the Firestone Library at Princeton University. She has also envisioned new library facilities for Colorado College, Syracuse University, and the New School University.

Richard Bussell's technical expertise spans IT, communications engineering, audiovisual systems design, and technology project management. He has strong business management skills, drawing from formal studies as well as his experience as principal of a large multidisciplinary architectural engineering firm. His formal qualifications include an undergraduate degree in communications engineering, a graduate degree in applied acoustics, and successful completion of the Advanced Management Program at UC Berkeley Haas School of Business.

Richard is a founding partner at Vantage Technology Consulting Group, where he works with his clients to help them anticipate the impacts and opportunities associated with new and emerging technologies and to adapt their systems, organizations, and facilities planning to suit. Since opening its doors in 2000, Vantage has grown to twenty consultants working out of offices located in Boston and Los Angeles.

James (Jim) Duncan formerly served as director of the Information Commons at the University of Iowa's Hardin Library, a position he held for more than ten years. He currently serves as director of the Networking and Resource Sharing Unit of the Colorado State Library in Denver.

Charles Forrest has nearly thirty years of experience in academic and research libraries. After almost a decade with the University of Illinois libraries, both at the Chicago campus and downstate at the flagship campus in Urbana-Champaign, he moved to Emory University in 1988. He has held a series of administrative positions in the main library there, including director of Instructional Support Services and director of Planning and Budget. He is currently director of Library Facilities Management and Planning. While at Emory, Charles has participated in the renovation or construction of over 300,000 square feet of library space, including serving as library project manager for the renovation of the Asa Griggs Candler Library, the first LEED-certified renovation project on campus. He is active in the American Library Association, the Association of College and Research Libraries, and the Library Leadership and Management Association, and is a regular presenter at library conferences, institutes, and workshops.

Martin Halbert is a nationally recognized leader in digital libraries. His doctoral research and subsequent research projects have focused on exploring the future of research library services.

He is director of Digital Innovations at the Emory University General Libraries in Atlanta, Georgia. He provides a leadership role within the library for computer systems operations, development, planning, and integration. He led the campus-wide effort to establish the Emory University Information Commons in 1998.

Martin has served as principal investigator for grants and contracts totaling more than $4 million during the past five years, and has sponsored funding that enabled more than a dozen large scale collaborative projects between Emory and other institutions. He is also president of the MetaArchive Cooperative, an international digital preservation collaborative service for cultural memory organization. He established the MetaArchive Digital Preservation Network (www. MetaArchive.org), a consortium of universities acting in concert with the Library of Congress to preserve our cultural heritage as part of the National Digital Preservation Program. Martin has led many interinstitutional committees, including the National Science Digital Library Policy Committee and the Digital Library Federation Aquifer Services Working Group. He previously worked for Rice University, the University of Texas at Austin, and the IBM Corporation.

Joan K. Lippincott is the associate executive director of the Coalition for Networked Information (CNI), a joint project of the Association of Research Libraries (ARL) and EDUCAUSE. CNI, an institutional membership organization, advances the transformative promise of networked information technology for the advancement of scholarly communication and the enrichment of intellectual productivity. She has been with CNI since 1990. At CNI, Joan has provided leadership for programs such as New Learning Communities, Assessment of the Networked Environment, Working Together, and collaborative facilities and learning spaces. She has written articles and made presentations on such topics as networked information, learning spaces, collaboration among professional groups, assessment, and teaching and learning in the networked environment. Her chapter on "Net Generation Students and Libraries" in an EDUCAUSE book on Educating the Net Generation (www.educause.edu/educatingthenetgen) has received wide distribution. She is chair of the editorial board of College & Research Libraries News, and serves on the board of the Networked Digital Library of Theses and Dissertations (NDLTD).

Joan previously held positions at the libraries of Cornell University, George Washington University, Georgetown University, and SUNY at Brockport. In addition, she worked at the Research and Policy Analysis Division of the American Council on Education, and the National Center for Postsecondary Governance and Finance at the University of Maryland. Joan received her PhD in higher education policy, planning, and administration from the University of Maryland, her MLS from SUNY Geneseo, and an AB from Vassar College.

Elizabeth J. Milewicz is a doctoral student in the Institute of the Liberal Arts at Emory University, where she is studying changing library environments and academic library culture. Theories and methods from linguistic anthropology, institutional sociology, and histories of the book and reading inform her work, as well as her background in library science. In the course of her academic career, she has worked as an interlibrary loan, serials, and education reference librarian; instructed undergraduate students in composition, literature, and the history of reading; and collaborated with education scholars on the study of preservice teacher development and reading and writing among young children.

Crit Stuart is program director for Research, Teaching, and Learning for the Association of Research Libraries (ARL). The mission of this new program is to develop and implement imaginative and practical strategies that promote and facilitate the integration and use of research library resources and services throughout the research institution. Prior to taking the ARL position in May 2007, Stuart was associate director for public services at the Library and Information Center, Georgia Institute of Technology, Atlanta, Georgia. There he coordinated the evolution of "library as place," emphasizing enhancements to spaces, technologies, and services to support student productivity and success in a twenty-four-hour environment, and expanding practical partnerships between the library and students, faculty, and student support services. The library received the ACRL Award for Excellence in Academic Libraries, university library section, for 2007.

Carole C. Wedge, AIA, LEED AP, is president of Shepley Bulfinch Richardson & Abbott. Carole's considerable expertise as a planner and programmer has focused on the convergence of learning, teaching, and research environments integrated with a long-standing commitment to principles of sustainability. She received a bachelor's in environmental design from the University of Colorado and a bachelor's in architecture from the Boston Architectural Center.